The Practical Guide to Organising Events

The Practical Guide to Organising Events is a short, accessible and practical guide on how to successfully plan and organise a variety of event types in a wide range of contexts. The core sections of the text are logically structured around the key stages of event management – pre-event, on-site and post-event – offering essential practical insight and guidance throughout the whole process. Topics covered include proposal writing, budget, funding and sponsorship, health and safety, security and evaluation. This is a fundamental resource for all events management students running and organising an event as part of their degree programme. It is also a book for anybody who just happens to be tasked with organising an event such as an office party, a social networking event, Christmas party or family wedding. Based on experience, using real-life case studies and anecdotal examples, *The Practical Guide to Organising Events* ultimately makes the business of events management appealing, understandable and achievable.

Philip Berners graduated with a degree in hospitality management from the University of West London where he later returned as a lecturer in events management. He is presently teaching events management and researching for his doctorate on the development of the events industry in a post-communist society: a case study of Poland.

Philip spent ten years in Poland as an events consultant and founded an events training school in Warsaw. He also taught event management for Collegium Civitas University at the Palace of Culture and Science.

Philip has organised every genre of event in the UK, Italy, Portugal and Poland; he was venue manager at the London Hippodrome, Camden Palace and Thorpe Park; and he has been the in-house event manager for corporations including the Daily Mail Group. His client portfolio includes the Queen, Prince Charles, Bon Jovi, Shania Twain, Jennifer Lopez, The BRIT Awards, MOBO Awards, *The Publican* newspaper, London Fashion Week, the British Red Cross, Xerox, Virgin

Atlantic, British Airways, Formula 1, Panasonic, *Max Power* magazine, *PC Zone* magazine, Alternative Hair Show, Kent Institute of Art and Design, Schweppes and Diageo.

Philip's qualifications are as follows: Bachelor of Arts Degree in Hospitality Management; City and Guilds in Hotel, Catering and Institutional Management; Postgraduate Certificate in Academic Practice; Fellowship of the Higher Education Academy; and he is about to commence his PhD.

The Practical Guide to Organising Events

Philip Berners

Routledge
Taylor & Francis Group

LONDON AND NEW YORK

First published 2017
by Routledge
2 Park Square, Milton Park, Abingdon, Oxon OX14 4RN

and by Routledge
711 Third Avenue, New York, NY 10017

Routledge is an imprint of the Taylor & Francis Group, an informa business

British Library Cataloguing in Publication Data
A catalogue record for this book is available from the British Library

Library of Congress Cataloging in Publication Data
A catalog record for this book has been requested

ISBN: 978-0-415-78998-1 (hbk)
ISBN: 978-0-415-78996-7 (pbk)
ISBN: 978-1-315-21363-7 (ebk)

Typeset in Iowan Old Style
by Florence Production Ltd, Stoodleigh, Devon, UK

Printed and bound in Great Britain by
TJ International Ltd, Padstow, Cornwall

I dedicate this book to two inspirational artists who entered my life:

Olaf Olenski

and

the late Whitney Houston

Contents

Contributors

Chantal Dickson is a senior lecturer in Events Management at Leeds Beckett University. Prior to joining LBU, Chantal worked in Australia primarily in the business event management and community event management sectors.

Ashley Garlick is senior lecturer in Event Management at the University of West London and was previously senior lecturer in Tourism and Events Management at London Metropolitan University. He has an undergraduate degree in International Hospitality Management and a Master's degree in Management, and has presented at academic conferences on the use of social media in learning environments. He is working on a PhD to research the symbolic meaning applied to strategy objects in organisations. Ashley's professional background includes ten years' experience working in live music events and licensed retail. He is also currently a volunteer manager with St John Ambulance, where he leads teams who volunteer at some of the largest events in the UK.

Paul Glover is a business consultant and restaurant owner. Prior to this, Paul was brand manager and account director for multinational advertising agencies. He has worked for over 30 years on global brands in Europe and the United States of America.

Ariane Lengyel was born in Paris, France. After graduating from Glion Institute of Higher Education, Ariane started her career in the resort of Cannes, and was then given the opportunity to go to the South Pacific island of Tahiti before moving to Hua-Hin in Thailand. She worked in rooms division in hotels for over ten years before moving to the UK and pursuing her career in head office sales and marketing for Accor Hotels. In 2008 she made a change into hospitality education. She holds a Master's in Culinary Arts Management and is a Senior Fellow of the Higher Education Academy. In 2016 she joined BPP University, London as programme leader for Hospitality and Events, and continues her research interests in the field of the sociology of food with a focus on celebrity chefs, presenting papers at several conferences.

Amira Malek graduated with a degree in Events Management from the University of West London. After graduating, Amira secured a position with a creative events company based in West London. She is involved with creating events around the world – mainly within the video games and technology sector.

Dr. Evangelia Marinakou has extensive teaching experience at undergraduate and postgraduate levels in various programmes in higher education following a career in management in the Greek hospitality industry. She has worked as events organiser and sales manager for tour operators in Greece, where she organised large conferences and other significant events. She has served as head of department and dean at various academic institutions in Greece, Switzerland, Bahrain and the UK. Her research interests focus on women in hospitality management and leadership, as well as teaching and learning methodologies in higher education. On these research areas she has published a book, book chapters and journal articles, and has presented at international conferences. She has also worked on European Union-funded projects as project leader with a focus on vocational training in hospitality and tourism. Moreover, she has trained a number of professionals in the industry in lifelong learning programmes. She is a reviewer in reputable academic journals and an accredited member of the Higher Education Academy.

David Titley: upon graduating with a degree in Events Management, David Titley was elected to the office of President of the University of West London Student's Union (UWLSU) by a majority 60% vote. Although his role is not event-based, David oversees a large team who organise many student activities including events for up to 500 guests. In his previous role at Twickenham Stadium, David was responsible for the hospitality for the BMW sponsor's lounge on major match days and he managed the catering operations for international media during the Rugby World Cup when his large team served 500 guests each day for a month.

Preface

My career path is unusual in its diversity because I did not remain in one sector of the industry, such as running venues or organising business conferences. I have moved around a lot and gained experience of every aspect of events management.

I have produced events, managed venues, been employed as the in-house head of events for large corporations, was the director of an event agency, spent ten years as an events consultant in Eastern Europe, and now I find myself lecturing future generations of event organisers.

During my career, I have organised most types of events, including parties, conferences, product launches, awards ceremonies, sports tournaments, weddings, exhibitions, fashion shows, concerts and film premieres. My client portfolio ranges from Xerox, Virgin Atlantic and British Airways to Her Majesty Queen Elizabeth II, His Royal Highness the Prince of Wales, Bon Jovi, Jennifer Lopez and Shania Twain. Somewhere along the way, I have been involved with The BRIT Awards, MOBO Awards and London Fashion Week.

The diversity of my career in the events industry means I have learnt an enormous amount about the art and practice of managing events.

Now, the most frequent question that is asked of me is how to reach the upper echelons in this exciting industry. To this question, I answer that it takes experience, not study.

This may seem odd, considering I teach events management. But, what a student wishes to learn in the classroom is the way of doing events. Unfortunately, the available textbooks tend to oversimplify the subject, or overcomplicate it. In truth, events management – like most careers – is not so easy, nor so difficult. It fits somewhere between. That is where *The Practical Guide to Organising Events* is different: it is written between study and experience. It fits between doing the job and studying the job. What I felt was needed was a practical guide to know how to do the job of organising events.

Philip Berners, BA PG Cert FHEA
London, 2016

Acknowledgements

The following have earned my thanks:

Professor David Foskett MBE CMA and Professor Ryszard Zoltaniecki for their inspiration going back many years.

Mr Ashley Garlick for contributing his knowledge to the sections on volunteers and marketing.

Ms Chantal Dickson, Mr Paul Glover, Ms Ariane Lengyel and Dr Evangelia Marinakou for contributing case studies, and Mr David Titley for contributing his reflections.

Ms Emma Travis at Routledge for commissioning this book.

Mr (Frederick) Brian Cook and Ms Anita Cook.

PART 1

Introduction

Chapter **1**

The culture of events

1.1 Developed markets

In developed markets, events management has evolved as an industry in itself and provides clients and corporations with services, facilities and management for putting on an event.

For anybody who has an event to run, there are directories that provide listings of event organisers, production companies, event services, caterers, venues, theme companies, prop hire, and music and entertainment.

Competition is fierce in developed markets: venues are vying for business and event organisers compete for clients. There is much overlap and anybody outside the events industry could be confused by the difference between an event management company, a production company or a public relations (PR) company.

1.1.1 Event management company

An event management company will provide its expertise for creative and themed events, such as parties, product launches and celebrations. They organise most elements for the running of an event, such as theme and decoration, creative concepts, budget management, venue sourcing, and liaison with suppliers and contractors. They take care of guest lists and will be there on the day of the event to provide operational management.

1.1.2 Production company

A production company specialises in events that require detailed technical elements, such as business conferences (projection, visuals and presentation speakers) and concerts (sound, light and special effects).

1.1.3 Public relations company or marketing company

These PR and marketing specialists provide the client with ideas and strategies that fit the promotional goals and brand fit of the organisation. The PR or marketing company would then employ the services of an event management company or a production company to execute the event.

The key identifier here – in regard to a developed event industry – is the employment of specialist companies to perform specialist tasks. The first mistake (which is endemic in undeveloped and developing markets) is using the wrong company for the wrong task – employing a marketing company to produce an event, say.

Confusion about the events industry is further driven because a large and complex event would necessitate the services of an event management company, a production company *and* a public relations company working alongside each other to achieve the goal of producing a successful event. The event management company will control the logistics and perform operational management at the event; the production company will take care of the technical requirements, such as staging and projection; and the PR or marketing company will send out invitations, draw up table plans, collate guest responses and manage the guest lists on the door at the event.

Consequently, there is a lot of crossover in the events industry and lines do get blurred as to who is responsible for which parts of an event (see Figure 1).

The events industry in developed markets can be likened to the medical profession. An optometrist does the eyes and a dentist does the teeth. You do not want the wrong one to do the other thing and you do not want one to do both!

Put simply, it is essential to recruit the correct specialist for the right job.

Figure 1 Interaction of event organisers at one event

In many cases, larger charities and large corporations have a need to organise many events. Rather than continuously outsourcing events management expertise, they have found it necessary to establish their own in-house events department that fits alongside the sales, marketing and PR functions, in which case the in-house head of events takes the responsibility for managing an event instead of the marketing manager.

It can be seen how events management in developed markets has become a recognised and established career path, and universities offer specialised courses to meet the demand.

1.2 Undeveloped and developing markets

In undeveloped and developing markets, the structure of the events industry is noticeably flat. At best, events are a responsibility added to the duties of an already overworked assistant in the marketing department. At worst, somebody can be tasked with the difficult job of organising an event, simply because 'they get on with people and are good at that sort of thing'.

In undeveloped and developing markets, few, if any, specialised event companies exist. Those that do exist have limited or no access to quality training and quality experience in the art of managing events, so the way they organise events evolves in a local fashion, which most often cannot achieve professionalism.

Furthermore, in undeveloped and developing markets event organisers are bereft of international experience. This can lead to their belief that they are managing events in the right manner, but without benchmarks to evidence this belief.

The lack of international experience is double-edged. On one side the event organiser will not understand how to approach international standards, and on the other side they may be contracted by a domestic client needing their services to produce an event abroad.

The absence of international expertise also presents the question of how undeveloped and developing markets can reach – even understand and appreciate – international levels of events management. Thus, a second tier of events management is created in these countries, which could be substandard in relation to international expectations. This causes problems when international clients – and guests – do not have their expectations met.

In most undeveloped and developing markets, the task of organising an event is outsourced to PR and marketing companies that are not event specialists. This drives an 'I do it all' culture where promises are made that may or may not be fulfilled. But, never mind the consequences because the priority is to secure the client's business, regardless. In this case, the factors of reputation and client retention do not appear to matter.

Training in the specialism of organising events in undeveloped and developing markets is limited to personal experience of the individual, which can be narrow, half-hearted or even wrong. But, this is all they know.

In such markets a career in event management can follow a haphazard pathway and will often occur by accident. This is where the study of events management meets experience: experienced event organisers can teach how to organise events.

Interestingly, events are vital in both developed and developing markets – it appears to be the career opportunities that differ. So, the professionalism and creativity of events differ vastly also. There simply is not the ability to create amazing events in undeveloped and developing markets and it is easier to follow the norm. The attitude tends to be 'this is the way we have always done it'.

But, all markets are increasingly global, not domestic, which means international standards are necessary to achieve.

The trend for events is becoming national, international and global: take for example the Euro 2012 football tournament hosted by Poland and Ukraine; Azerbaijan hosting the Eurovision Song Contest; the Brazil Olympics; the Qatar World Cup . . .

AUTHOR'S VOICE BOX

In a developing market, I know of a successful fashion designer who organises every detail of his own catwalk shows.

At one event, the bar was placed in the wrong location at the venue – it was not visible to guests, which was a wasted opportunity. But, also the drinks sponsor lost the exposure of their products to the audience.

When I pointed out this logistical error to the talented designer at a meeting a week or so after his show, he took personal offence because *he* had decided where the bar should be positioned.

But, how could a fashion designer know the complexities and pitfalls of organising events such as where a bar should be placed – and why should he need to know?

This situation underlines the point that expertise in events is necessary. After all, as an event organiser, I would not attempt to design a dress.

International audiences have expectations of experience, quality, standards and safety. Low standards equate to high risk, and this is no longer good enough for the global audience.

1.3 Sustainable events

With the growth in the number of events happening in both developed and developing markets, coupled with the growth in the size of actual events, sustainability is a growing issue also.

Guests and visitors possess an increasing expectation when attending events that are designed to provide them with an experience, that it is also a good experience for the environment.

Where social events such as music festivals attract young and socially aware visitors, there is demand for socially aware practices. It is becoming increasingly unacceptable to offer a guest-experience at the cost of the environment.

So, the event organiser must meet guest demands and expectations – as always. This requires sourcing innovative and forward-looking solutions for the legacy of an event and the impact it leaves behind.

Where massive events now happen, the key sustainable areas to consider are waste clearance; distance of travel necessary for both visitors to the event and the suppliers so as to lessen carbon impact; land recovery; and power sources. The latter should be solar and wind-generated where possible. Temporary toilet facilities can be sawdust-based to absorb fluid waste instead of needing to transport large quantities of raw waste to external processing sites.

The motivation to create an environmentally friendly event is led by guest demands and expectations. But this alone is not enough. It is easy to employ marketing tactics to pretend sustainability and the guests will never know the true 'cost' to the planet.

Legislation is the true motivator, but the law on sustainable events is lacking. Finally, then, the motivating factor to produce a sustainable event is that of reducing costs. Financial incentives are helping to deliver sustainability and event organisers are sourcing cheaper alternatives for the provision of power and the disposal of waste, which is drawing the event industry towards sustainable solutions.

Chapter **2**

The structure of events

What is an event?

An event is *any live happening*.

There it is: the definition of an event in just three words.

A hurricane is an event: a *live happening* defined as being a weather event. An earthquake is a live happening: a natural event. A train crash is a live happening: defined as being a catastrophic event.

Event management, therefore, is about managing a live event so that it does not turn out to be a train wreck.

This book is about *the management of live happenings*.

If we could manage a hurricane, an earthquake or a train wreck, we would. We would assess the risks of such an event – where it would happen; how many people would be affected; what is the severity of the catastrophe about to happen – and measures could be put in place to minimise injury and harm. We could move people to shelters and emergency rescue teams could be deployed in the exact area of the event before it occurs. Of course, we would require notice of the event – early warning systems, such as for tsunamis, go some way to forecasting warnings – and it would then require planning in meticulous detail to minimise risk. Planning does take time. This is called the *lead-in*. Although disasters are sometimes forecast and planning is achievable to a degree – to shore up windows or evacuate the vulnerable, perhaps – it is always a sudden and emergency situation, so the lead-in is limited. When we are planning an event, we can plan how much time we need to bring all elements together before the day of the event.

So, the amount of lead-in can be planned – we have this luxury. If we do not plan the event and if we do not calculate the lead-in period during which the planning takes place, a train wreck it will be.

The job of the event manager is to minimise risk.

2.1 Types of event

Managed events occur in many forms and for many different objectives. So, it is necessary to understand the differences between one event and another.

2.1.1 Functions

Functions are smaller events. Usually, they are uncomplicated and follow a standard format, such as a dinner, wedding or drinks reception. They can be formal or informal and would normally be held in a venue that is intended for the purpose, such as a function room or a hotel banqueting suite.

2.1.2 Productions

Productions are events that contain technical requirements and as such are complex. They require technical expertise – a production company. Concerts, presentations, awards ceremonies and stage shows fit into this category of event. The technicians who organise whatever happens on stage are the *production crew*.

The *production company* might additionally manage the event if their expertise is not limited only to technical elements, but is diverse enough to manage other elements of an event, and if the event is not considered major enough to require the support of additional specialist event management expertise.

2.1.3 Banquets

Banquets are sit-down dinners and are formal, such as mayoral, military and regimental occasion dinners. This type of event follows a standard format, usually with arrival drinks, then the banquet, followed by dancing. Typically, formal attire is required unless the invitation stipulates informal dress. The style of food service can vary between plate service, family service and silver service (see

6.1.4.2), but always the seating would be grouped on round tables or square tables, or according to a 'sprig' layout where tables branch off the long 'top' table. A formal wedding would also be considered as a banquet.

2.1.4 Galas

Galas are the same as banquets, but with a show or stage presentation. The emphasis is on entertainment, whereas the emphasis of a banquet is the dining occasion.

2.1.5 Conferences

Conferences are business meetings that are designed to deliver a message to a target audience, or *delegates*, who attend the conference either by choice or requirement. These events can be a press conference for a company to impart information to the media; a sales presentation to a company's sales force; or a pharmaceutical conference to demonstrate a new medical product to doctors.

Conferences tend to follow a standard format, as in Table 1.

It is not unusual to omit some of the requirements listed here, for instance by not having an afternoon coffee break, or not having any evening activity.

Table 1 Typical conference format

Morning	Arrival
	Registration
	Badge each delegate with a name-badge
	Arrival tea, coffee, juices, pastries
	Conference commences
Mid-morning	Break
	Tea, coffee, juices, biscuits
	Conference recommences
Lunchtime	Lunch
Afternoon	Conference recommences
Mid-afternoon	Break
	Tea, coffee, juices, biscuits
	Conference recommences
Late afternoon	Conference ends
	Post-conference networking reception with drinks and buffet
	or
	Evening dinner with entertainment / dancing / awards

The all-inclusive charge for room hire, teas and coffees, and lunch is typically presented as a package and can be divided by the number of delegates attending the conference to ascertain the *delegate rate* (charge per delegate).

The delegate rate can also include accommodation if this is a requirement. If an evening reception, party or dinner is part of the brief, then this can be itemised separately to show the cost, or it could be incorporated within the delegate rate to show the cost per delegate for all the requirements.

Conference and business meetings often require *breakout rooms* to allow workshop groups, discussion groups or project groups to meet outside the main conference hall.

2.1.6 Exhibitions

Exhibitions are for the purpose of displaying or showcasing products and services, where numerous independent exhibitors pay for their stand or space in the exhibition hall.

An exhibition will be for the purpose of awareness, so that exhibitors can generate sales leads. It should be noted that sales are not always necessary to achieve *during* all exhibitions. Data capture from visitors is a key objective of exhibitors, so they can follow up sales leads after the exhibition has ended.

Also, a lot of people attend exhibitions for networking and awareness, rather than doing business.

Closed or *trade-only* exhibitions are not open to the public, but they are still sales-oriented, just to a targeted market, industry or interested parties.

Many exhibitions have related activities happening during the exhibition period, such as personal appearances, keynote speakers, demonstrations, book signings, lectures and exhibitor parties or dinners. Some have awards events and gala dinners for attendees. Such activities work because the target market comes together at one location for the exhibition. It also adds value and kudos to the occasion of the exhibition.

2.1.7 Launches

Launches are a category of event that is wide and varied, and can include Formula 1 team launches at the beginning of the racing season, new record album releases, new products, rebranded products, the latest cars, fashion collections or shop openings. Launches can be creative and exciting events to organise, especially if they are high profile and have celebrities and press attending.

2.1.8 Fashion shows

Fashion shows are organised to showcase a designer's forthcoming collection to fashion buyers and the fashion media. They usually occur twice a year to show spring/summer (SS) and autumn/winter (AW) collections.

Although fashion shows follow a standard format, clothes designers are fiercely competitive and seek ways to introduce creative differences into their shows. Many times, fashion shows are staged in impressive or unusual venues.

Fashion show venues are usually required to accommodate a long stage, called a *catwalk* (or *runway*), for the models to parade the clothes. Also, there must be good and spacious backstage facilities for changing rooms, clothes hanging, hairdressers and make-up artists.

As a rule, white light is hung directly above the catwalk, so this requires good ceiling height. There must also be space for the audience, including seated and front-row guests.

2.1.9 Premieres

Premieres are for film releases and theatre debuts. Of course, a film would be premiered in a cinema, and a play or musical would be debuted in a theatre. Afterwards, the invited guests would attend a reception, dinner or party, which would usually be styled to the theme of the film, play or musical. The after-show event may be in the same venue or close by.

Premieres are attended by the cast, so they do attract press interest. Often, they are attended by royalty (a *royal premiere*), in which case the premiere event will be in support of the royal patron's charity.

2.1.10 Screenings

Screenings are events to show a film, which may be a private viewing for the press or critics prior to general release, or it could be a series of screenings during a film festival. A screening may also be a public event to show a film for a limited period, such as the screening of a cult, retro or vintage film.

2.1.11 Parties

Parties are just fun!

2.2 Sectors of the event industry

In addition to the aforementioned types of events, the event industry can be categorised by sectors.

2.2.1 Corporate events

Corporate events can be defined as such because the corporation is paying the bill. Therefore, the event is being organised on behalf of a business client.

Corporate events are not necessarily formal – take a corporate fun day at a theme park, for example, where the corporation entertains its employees, clients or guests.

Even so, corporate events are for business purposes, or are being organised on behalf of a business client.

2.2.2 Public events

Public events are open to members of the public, even though attendance may not be free and can be restricted to ticket-holders only (but is not always).

A public event could be a concert, music festival, county show or a street festival such as Notting Hill Carnival.

These events could be in a venue or in the open.

2.2.3 Charity events

Charity events are for the purpose of raising funds or awareness for a charity. In most cases, sponsors and donations are sought to limit the costs of the event, which the charity would otherwise need to pay. Sometimes, suppliers and even the event organiser are expected to donate their services and not take payment so as to optimise funds raised for the charity.

But, being a 'charity event' does not always mean it is an event with a low budget, even if the allocation of the budget is carefully managed. The largest and highest-profile events are, in most cases, supporting or promoting charities. Often, celebrities and royalty are affiliated with charities, which significantly raises the event's profile and the level of press interest, and makes for charity events being highly creative and exciting.

Celebrity endorsement is a common occurrence, particularly with charities, to raise the profile of the cause. There is nothing wrong with exploiting a well-known person's celebrity status – product advertisers do it all the time. Celebrities need the profile, too, and will endorse an event so that they attract press themselves and are associated with the good cause of the charity.

> **AUTHOR'S VOICE BOX**
>
> I was asked to write a consultancy paper for a charity committee.
>
> One of my recommendations was for the charity to recruit a celebrity to raise the profile of their cause.
>
> Unfortunately, the committee rejected the proposal outright because they were nervous of attracting adverse publicity if the celebrity were to do something wrong in the public eye.
>
> Celebrities do 'wrong' things all the time, and either the charity must at that point distance themselves from the wrong situation, or they must rescind the celebrity's endorsement. Or, they should simply enjoy the raised profile of their charity.

2.2.4 Trade events

Trade events are for the attendance of people who work in a particular industry. Mainly, conferences and exhibitions fall into this category.

Such events are not open to the public (except if there are designated press days, student days or public days).

Farnborough International Airshow is a good example of a trade event, where the show is open only to trade visitors on Monday to Thursday, students on Friday and then the general public on Saturday and Sunday.

2.2.5 Press events

Press events can be any of the aforementioned types of events, but with the objective of informing or entertaining the press, so that they may write favourably about the event, product or service.

As the press can attend any event, a designated *press event*, such as a press conference, is usually organised solely for communicating with the media.

2.3 The structure of an event

Having understood the various types of events and the structure of the events industry, we can look in greater detail at the structure of an event.

2.3.1 Event objectives

Every event is born from the need to meet an objective.

The objective for holding an event can be to raise awareness about a new product and generate sales interest from guests, such as for a music album release. Or, the objective could be the need to entertain clients and staff at a Christmas party. It could be to disseminate information to the company's sales force at a conference, or it may be to showcase a designer's new collection to the fashion industry. Or, the event objective could simply be to make money from selling tickets to attend a public concert or exhibition.

Whatever the event, and whatever the objectives are, an event is designed to reach people or to make money.

There is always a client which will be a corporation, a charity, or even a private individual in the cases of a wedding or birthday party.

The client is in charge of setting the event's objectives, although sometimes the client does not identify the objectives or know what they are.

Then, there must be an event organiser who is responsible for achieving the event's objectives. So, if the client does not know the objectives, the event organiser must either use their experience to understand why the event is happening, or question the client at the briefing stage to ascertain the objectives.

The event organiser might be employed by the corporation or charity that is holding the event, and thus would be an in-house event manager or in-house head of events and would be the 'client' in the eyes of the venue and other event suppliers.

Or, the event organiser could be the event manager at a venue, and thus would be the venue manager or venue head of events and not the client.

Or, the event organiser could be a hired specialist, and thus would be a freelance event manager or would work at an event agency, and the client would be the person who engages his services.

As well as a client and an event organiser, there are contractors, suppliers and service providers. These are the caterers, sound and light technicians, stage crew, flower arrangers, entertainment, decorators, the disc jockey, security staff, the waiters, furniture hire companies, marquee companies and every other provider of whatever goes into making the event.

It is important for the client to set the objectives, and the event organiser must ensure the objectives do not clash.

> **AUTHOR'S VOICE BOX**
>
> There was a fashion show organised for young designers to showcase their talent. The event was staged in a BMW showroom.
>
> It was clear that BMW were sponsoring the event and had provided the venue for free so they could capitalise on the fashionable audience, celebrities and press attending the fashion event and unveil the latest BMW at the same time.
>
> Carefully managed and orchestrated, this joint event could have worked very nicely. The car reveal should have happened at the beginning of the fashion show, to 'launch' both the car and the opening of the show.
>
> And, the gleaming new car could have been positioned at the end of the catwalk, because it was a new 'model' as well. The photo opportunities and branding would have worked perfectly.
>
> However, the fashion show took place on one side of the auto showroom and the car reveal was on the other. So, they competed with each other in a venue built for cars.
>
> Some of the audience were seated at the side of the catwalk and were trapped, but craned their necks to see what was happening at the other end of the venue and see what they were missing!
>
> It was difficult to know which event was the climax – the fashion show or the car launch. It felt like two clients, two events, too many objectives and a half-and-half approach.
>
> And, it appeared cheap because two events were sharing one budget.

2.3.2 The venue

The place where an event is held is termed as the 'venue'. If the event is held in a venue built for the purpose of hosting events (a hotel or conference centre, say), the contractors and service providers will largely be in-house and provided by the venue. However, if the event is happening in a warehouse, disused building, an unusual venue or an open *green-field* space, then the requirements become much more complex and need to be brought on-site: they have to be sourced externally. Power and heating may be required, as may mobile toilet facilities, water, trackways for access by people and vehicles, staging, kitchens, staff and security.

This is where the lead-in time must be calculated as to how much planning is needed, and is also why the size of an event team varies for each event. It can be a large or small team. The event may or may not warrant security, technicians or staging. It may require an event company *and* a production company to work alongside each other. But, even a straightforward event with a small team, and held in a purpose-built venue, requires an event organiser. And, if the event is *guaranteed* to be a success, it must have a good event organiser.

Chapter  **3**

The role of the event organiser

An event organiser must delegate to a team and trusted suppliers.

3.1 Types of event organiser

There are three types of event organiser.

3.1.1 In-house

This is someone *within* an organisation who is charged with the responsibility of managing all the company's events. This may be a knowledgeable and experienced event organiser, such as the in-house head of events. It could, however, be a person who organises events as part of their role as the marketing or PR manager. Or, it may be an employee with limited event experience – a secretary, personal assistant, or somebody who got the job of organising the event simply because they are good with people and are popular with all the staff.

3.1.2 External specialist

A lot of companies do not have an event organiser. And, even where they do, this person may require the additional support of the second type of event organiser: an *external specialist* event organiser.

The external specialist will be trained and experienced in the management of events and will not only provide the company's internal event organiser with additional ideas and technical know-how, but quite often the internal organiser is already busy with other responsibilities and may not be in a position to dedicate the time and focus that an event demands.

This second type of event organiser – the external specialist – may be freelance or could be working at an event management company or agency. They will be in a position to propose the event concept, construct the budget, then execute the event using their specialist experience and trusted industry contacts and suppliers.

3.1.3 Venue event manager

The third type of event organiser is the one employed at the venue. Venues that are busy with events will have an event management team to manage enquiries and convert them into sales, manage client accounts and relations, manage the event logistics and ensure their clients' expectations and needs are met.

Typically, the team would be fronted by a head of events, and supported by an event manager and event co-ordinators.

But, even venues that are not busy with events may have an event manager on their team for the occasions when events occur and to handle the enquiry and booking procedures, and for marketing their facilities to the corporate events sector. Otherwise, the general manager or marketing manager will carry these duties within their role.

For the purposes of ease and clarity of the various types of event manager, henceforward this role will be referred to as the *event organiser*.

Generally, the size and complexity of the event determines the level of management input required to plan the event and organise the logistics.

The busy marketing assistant organising the office Christmas party may do everything herself. But, even if it is a simple event, she may choose a venue that has experience of organising events and has a venue event manager, who can manage the logistics for her and release her from the burden.

On the other hand, a corporation that is organising a large and complex event that has a high media and celebrity profile as well, may have an *internal* event manager who employs the services of a trusted *external* event specialist, who places the event at a venue that has a *venue event manager*. In such cases there are three event organisers for the one event, which is not unusual (see Figure 2).

3.2 The 'real' event manager

There is often more than one event organiser at an event because there will at the very least be a client and a venue manager, but there could additionally be

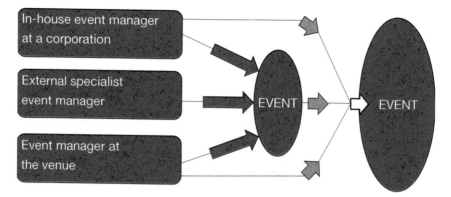

Figure 2 The three types of event manager may work independently, or they may come together and work alongside each other for a larger or more complex event

the external specialist, sponsors, and a marketing company. Each will believe they are the decision maker: the event organiser. This can cause conflict, so it is helpful to identify who is the 'real' event manager.

The event specialist is the most knowledgeable and experienced, so could be identified as the real event manager.

But, when the event specialist walks into a venue and meets the venue manager, it is *not* the specialist who is most knowledgeable and experienced about that venue. Only the venue manager knows the idiosyncrasies of that venue. There will be health and safety risks pertinent to that particular venue. The venue manager will know what works in that venue and what does not work. So, it is clearly the venue manager who becomes the real event manager.

And, when the production manager comes on-site for a meeting to discuss technical arrangements, *he* is the most knowledgeable and experienced in the specialism of technical arrangements, so *he* becomes the real event manager. It is not for the event specialist to decide technical arrangements, nor is it the role of the venue manager. It is the optometrist and the dentist again – which specialist to use for the job.

Similarly, when the client arrives on-site and makes decisions about the event, the client is most knowledgeable about what is acceptable. So now the client becomes the real event manager.

It can be seen that the 'real' event manager is a transient role. It passes back and forth, and can do so fluidly and constantly.

If the event specialist learns to identify and accept who is the real event manager in all situations, there is little risk of conflict by everybody believing they are the person in charge; the one who calls the shots; the 'client'.

This trick will avoid much conflict and upset, and is surprisingly simple to enact.

All it takes is the understanding of the principle of advice – *providing* advice when in the position of the real event manager, and *accepting* advice from other people when they are the most knowledgeable and experienced in their field so *they* become the real event manager.

After all, the client is paying the bill and making the decisions, but the client will need advising by the venue and the event specialists. Clients tend to dream big and may not know the pitfalls of their dreams – they are not event professionals, which is why they need a venue and/or an event specialist. So, if the rule of the real event manager is enacted, the client will seek advice and will accept it, and nobody will be in conflict by attempting to prove they know best about how to organise the event.

3.3 The 'real' client

The company's internal event organiser is 'the client', because they are paying the bill, which naturally makes them the decision maker.

However, the venue will consider the external event specialist as being their client, because the specialist would probably have recommended the venue. Anyway, the specialist is the liaison point for the venue. Also, it may be the specialist who controls the client's budget and is therefore paying the venue bill.

Then there are the contractors, such as caterers, whom the venue brings in and who may have an established and loyal relationship with the venue. These contractors will view the venue as their client.

If contractors are brought in by the external event organiser, they will refer to this person as their client, because this person contracted them, will pay their bill and may have an established and loyal relationship with them.

On top of this, there can be other stakeholders, such as sponsors, who have client expectations themselves, so they believe they are the client – after all, they are donating funds or product for the event to happen.

There can be a lot of 'clients'.

To get around the problem of the event organiser having so many clients to deal with, it is advantageous to apply the same principle as the real event manager, and identify who the 'real' client is. This can be done in the same way, by addressing each 'client' for their particular area of interest. In other words, when dealing with the sponsor's issues, the sponsor is the real client. However, when dealing with contractors, they become the real client.

It would be an error to allow the client to be the client for the event organiser, plus the venue and contractors. If this were to happen and the client were to assume power, decisions would be made between parties outside the event organiser.

So, when the event organiser is dealing with his client, this client is the 'real' client. This relationship must be nurtured and managed to ensure closeness, trust and loyalty so that the client does not seek guidance direct from the venue or other contracted parties.

The event organiser must develop a hierarchy where all 'clients' channel their communication to him, the 'real' client, whilst respecting that other parties perceive other clients. Failure to do this introduces lack of control, and risk.

This is an important rule to observe because the event organiser does not want the venue dealing direct with the client if they perceive that relationship to exist.

Neither does the event organiser want the client making arrangements direct with the venue.

If the principle of identifying who the 'real' client is in any situation is properly followed, the client will naturally liaise with the event organiser, and the event organiser will be able to manage each 'client' relationship.

With individual private clients, such as parents organising their daughter's wedding, the client/event manager relationship is straightforward.

Most likely, the parents will not seek an events specialist, but will simply place the event at a venue where there is an event manager. This will be because the parents are not experienced in event management and will rely solely upon the venue's experience and expertise for the success of the event.

However, the venue event manager must be careful to adopt the 'real client' rule. Otherwise, the bride's mother will be making arrangements with the florist, the photographer and the cake specialist, and these contractors will treat that lady as their real client. And all this will happen outside the control of the event organiser. If this were to happen, elements will occur on the day, of which the event organiser was unaware. This close management of the client also allows the event organiser to liaise directly with approved suppliers which may generate a commission.

3.4 Risk and control

The remit of the event organiser is straightforward, even if it is not simple: it is to ensure the smooth running of a live happening.

This is achieved by eliminating – or certainly minimising – risk.

The reason the event organiser's job is not a simple remit is that event management begins at least three months prior to the date of the event. In fact, the *lead-in* period can be anything up to a year before the event happens. This is *pre-event* management.

Then, the job continues throughout the duration of the event – *on-site* or *operational* event management.

And, it extends to after the event – *post-event* or *after-event* management.

It is a job that requires skill in administration, financial control, creativity, vision, organisation skills, team leadership, human resource management, motivation skills, delegation, decision making, problem solving and attention to detail.

Further, it is a job that requires the essential ability to draw together many components to achieve the objective of a successful event.

The event organiser is at the top of the pyramidal organisational structure, with all components of the event and all those who are responsible for each component reporting to the event organiser.

Above all, nothing must happen without the event organiser knowing it, expecting it, and having planned for it.

Nothing is gifted to chance. This is planning.

So, the good event organiser must be a 'control freak'. This is what the job demands. Such a label, if applied, should not be taken as a jibe, but should be treated as confirmation of doing the job well.

This does not mean that the event organiser must *do* everything – delegation is one of the key skills. It is important to let other people carry out their specialist jobs. By doing so, the event organiser is free to oversee every element of the event, and not focus on individual elements, which is the responsibility of team members.

But, the event organiser must be in *control* of everything that is happening and everybody who is charged with making it happen.

Even if one small component of a large event can be allowed to go wrong because it is outside the *control* of the event organiser, imagine the risk with a larger component, such as using an unknown caterer.

It is imperative for the event organiser to have a relationship of trust and confidence with all contractors, caterers and service suppliers that will be used to ensure the event is a success. *They* are the reputation of a good event organiser when the event is a success.

AUTHOR'S VOICE BOX

To highlight the need for the event organiser to control every component of the event, I cite an album release which I was asked to organise.

My client insisted upon using a known London disc jockey for the album release party. I cautioned the client because the style of music of this particular DJ did not suit the style of music of the band who were releasing the album.

Secretly, however, I felt unhappy for the music at the event to be provided by a DJ whom I didn't know. I knew it would place this component of the event out of my *control*.

Eventually, I relented because there were many other components for me to organise and I felt the DJ was a minor compromise for me to make.

That was my mistake.

On the evening of the event, the famous DJ missed his flight to the destination. He missed the rehearsal and the briefing.

When he 'spun his discs' everybody complained about the awful music. The guests – many of whom were VIPs – complained to me because I was the event organiser. It was embarrassing for me. But, the DJ was not under my control – I hadn't booked him or contracted him.

It became such a problem that I had to insist that the client pull the DJ from the decks.

It would have been unprofessional for me to shift the blame to my client, so I had to accept the blame. But, I did wish that I could tell everybody in the venue that I had advised against it and it was not my fault!

If I had used a DJ whom I knew and trusted, I would have known he would not arrive late – or I might have known he had a tendency to be late and would have planned for it. If he had been under my control and jurisdiction, and *I* were his client, I could have specified the style of music, the volume and everything else about the music at this event.

But, because I had allowed this 'minor' component to escape my control, I had failed. So, it was my fault, after all.

The event organiser must control every aspect of the event, and must know exactly what is going to happen, and when.

There must be no surprises.

Nothing must be allowed to happen without first being planned and approved by the event organiser. This way, nothing can be allowed to go wrong.

There is always the possibility of the unexpected, however. It does not mean the event was wrongly planned. It does mean that the event organiser must compensate for the unexpected.

The secret of good event management is in trusting the suppliers. They are the event organiser's reputation and legacy.

3.5 Staffing

The event organiser is not *doing* everything, of course. There will be the support of suppliers and contractors, and there will be an event management *team* as well.

Depending on the size and complexity of an event, the event organiser may be supported by an assistant event manager, production manager, sponsorship manager, administration and budget manager, venue manager, artist hospitality manager, catering manager and security manager.

AUTHOR'S VOICE BOX

My trusted technical manager carries a spare projector bulb on-site in case the first one fails. It is this level of planning and having faith in one's suppliers that provides the event organiser with the assurance that the event will not go wrong.

This same technical manager refuses to rely on Velcro to secure a logo to a podium or stage backdrop. He insists on inserting at least one screw to hold the item in place.

When I watched the President of the United States give a live television address to a global audience and the presidential seal fell from the lectern and rolled across the stage, I thought how *my* technical manager would not have allowed that to happen!

There will also be a team of supporting staff for any event. The staff may be employed by the venue (bar staff, waiters, security staff, cleaners, porters, technicians) or by the caterer (chefs, kitchen porters, waiters, porters). Or, the staff may be supplied direct to the event organiser by a staffing agency. There can be full-time, part-time and casual staff, the latter being staff who are drafted in for the job and get paid by the hour. These are usually the service staff such as bar and waiting staff, but can include crew and porters. Then, there are freelance staff who are usually self-employed specialists such as riggers and technical crew.

3.5.1 Volunteer staff

It used to be that charities were the domain for volunteers because of their need to reduce event costs such as labour, which possibly led to the misperception that charity events were low-budget events.

The more cost savings that can be made when putting on a charity event, the more contribution there will be to the charity coffers. As the purpose of most charity events is to raise funds (otherwise it will be to raise profile), it makes sense to keep the costs of a charity event to a minimum.

This becomes particularly relevant for large-scale charity events which require a sizeable team, such as marshals for challenge events ('challenge' events are those that challenge the participants. These, typically, are marathons, bike rides and sporting fundraisers).

Charities attract volunteers for a variety of reasons. It could be that the volunteer supports the cause, or wants to do something worthwhile with their spare time, wishes to meet like-minded people, or the cause of the charity has touched them in some way, either directly or through a friend or relative who has required the services of that charity.

Events outside the charity sector are now making use of volunteers as well. Large-scale events, festivals, challenge events and concerts seek to reduce the costs of an event by utilising volunteer staff.

Whereas charities motivate the participation of volunteers as previously identified, other events offer other motivations, such as: participation in an exciting event; experience; fun; teamwork; watching the performers; and receiving rewards other than financial ones, such as free travel, accommodation and meals.

Event organisers must understand that volunteers require motivation to provide their services and time for free. Key to this is the motivation of having a good experience, as this alone can retain volunteers to participate at repeat events, which is useful because most charity and large-scale events are staged annually.

3.5.2 Contribution from Ashley Garlick

Using volunteers

So you have decided to use volunteers for your event. The most important question you should now be asking yourself is: why? If the answer is that you are looking for easy, free labour then you should think again. As you will see in this section, using volunteers often requires more time and effort than using paid staff. And, while you do not have the direct cost of wages, it is by no means free.

A successful volunteer relationship is one based on mutual benefit. Using volunteers, especially if drawn from the local community, can engender a sense of ownership of the event by the community, resulting in an increased level of commitment. This can be especially beneficial if your event comes with some negative impacts on your immediate neighbours. For example, local residents may have their daily routine disrupted by increased traffic congestion, or may be 'land-locked' in their homes by road closures. An opportunity to be directly involved in the delivery of the event may help distract the local community from the annoyance your event generates.

Another important positive reason to use volunteers is the social value it can add; a great volunteering experience helps people feel good about themselves and their community. It can instil a sense of pride and ownership in the local area, as well as help build teams who may go on to work together on other projects.

When considering staffing arrangements, you should think about what it is you have to offer an individual wanting to be involved in your event. Perhaps you can provide opportunities for personal development, or a level of responsibility that is a step up from their paid job. You should particularly consider things that may be low-cost to you, but have a higher value for other people – such as free entry to this or a future event, or the use of your facilities at some other time.

If you find there is nothing of value to give, consider giving money, i.e. employing paid staff.

In order to understand what you may be able to offer others, it will help to understand why people volunteer in the first place.

Why do people volunteer?

The first thing to understand is that there are a range of different reasons why someone would provide their labour for free.

Volunteers will have many different reasons for wanting to be part of your event, which makes it difficult to consider them all.

Your volunteers may each have a combination of reasons, which may or may not be obvious when you take them on.

There are a number of common reasons why many people choose to give their time to an organisation. These are personal or professional development, altruism, utilising skills and receiving benefits in kind.

Volunteering can provide opportunities to gain experience that might not be possible to gain elsewhere. Therefore, people are attracted to events that might develop their skills or provide experience that may help them in future.

Events provide a wealth of different roles that test a range of skills, whether these be customer service skills, cash handling, communication, organisation, problem solving and many, many more. The experience gained by volunteering at events can help people develop their professional careers by helping gain valuable practice that can be used to enhance a CV or job application.

The implication of this, however, is that by providing someone with experience they do not already possess, you are inherently using volunteers to undertake roles in which they will not be experienced; your expectations in terms of how competent these volunteers will be must therefore reflect this. If you 'sell' a volunteering opportunity as one that would enhance a CV, then do not be surprised to attract low-skilled applicants.

There are a significant number of people who volunteer purely for the benefit of others. These selfless individuals give up their time without expectation of direct benefit to themselves. They will often be found working with charitable organisations, or directly for a particular cause which is important to them.

If you are running a commercial venture, you will find your profit margins are unlikely to count as an important cause, and so are unlikely to attract volunteers on purely altruistic terms, unless there are other goals that show a clear benefit to others.

For many people, volunteering is as much a hobby as a sport or gaming is to others. It provides an opportunity to utilise existing skills they may have, sometimes in new or novel environments. For example, doctors and nurses may enjoy providing medical cover at events because it allows them to use their valuable skills, but not in a hospital environment; this gets them to think about everyday professional issues from a new and sometimes unusual perspective.

There are many other rewards to be had from volunteering: free merchandise, free entry, free use of the on-site gym. This transactional approach to volunteering sees benefits for both parties, and should result in a 'win/win' situation because it generates mutual good.

The fantastic thing about events is that they are very highly valued by those who go to them; a few hours' work might be well worth a few hours at the event, so sometimes you can trade your own product. It is an exchange of want and need. And, the great thing about this is that it will usually cost you nothing.

Recruiting volunteers

Where you find volunteers, and how you select them, can be one of the biggest factors that will determine how successful they are as a contribution to the running of your event.

On its own, pay is unlikely to drive employees to do a good job; however, the prospect of pay can attract applicants and be an opportunity to motivate them. Without the reward of payment, volunteers must be attracted to other aspects of the role, and therefore these need to be very clearly communicated in any volunteer recruitment campaign.

Careful analysis of what roles you are looking for, and therefore what skills are needed, will be an important first step in recruiting the best and most suitable volunteers. Different roles are going to lend themselves to different types of volunteers. It cannot be assumed that volunteers should always fit the most unskilled positions. Sometimes, you may do better by utilising paid staff for some roles that, without the reward of payment, may otherwise be unappealing for anybody to undertake.

Volunteer positions often come with more responsibility than you might expect, as this is an attractive route for individuals who are looking to advance their careers, but need to gain more experience at a higher level to get a more responsible paid job. The advantage here is that you can attract skilled volunteers, who will be highly motivated to prove themselves and their abilities.

Jobs that are important on the event day but not required beforehand during the building of the event, nor afterwards during the break-down, such as team leaders, control room operators and artist liaison, can be great opportunities for volunteers to excel in their roles.

When you have identified the skills you are looking for, then you can start thinking about the type of person who might be attracted to those roles.

When you know the type of person you are looking for, then you can identify where you might find them.

If you are looking to engage the local community, look for groups you could approach such as residents' associations or youth groups. Perhaps put up a poster in the local pub or shop.

If you need people with specialist skills, consider colleges or universities that teach related courses.

If you are seeking volunteers with a strong interest and passion for the event, research clubs or societies that are involved in similar or related activities; for example, if you are organising a charity fun run then approach local running clubs. Even if the runners themselves are more interested in participating in the event rather than volunteering to help staff it, it may be that they have friends and family who would be keen to get involved and provide support in a more active way.

Before approaching potential volunteers, it is important to have a clear idea about exactly what you are asking for and the process they will need to follow. When giving up a significant amount of time for free, the least a volunteer can expect is certainty and detail about exactly what is involved. What are the times and dates they will be needed for? What tasks will they be expected to undertake? Will they be required to attend training before the event? Will their expenses be paid or not? What can they expect to get out of their experience? These are all reasonable questions that, if not included on the advertisement, may deter people from applying.

The application process should be clear and simple to follow. Should they express their interest by email, or provide a CV? Will there be a selection process or interview? When should they expect a response? There may be some common conventions to draw upon when applying for a job, but volunteering practices vary greatly, so make sure you provide as much information as possible.

Where you need a number of volunteers, and especially when you might want to use volunteers again in future, you should keep and maintain some basic documentation. A clear role description and person specification can help provide clear information to applicants, as well as give you an easy way to compare and select the most appropriate people. Keeping records of who applies, whether and why they were successful or not, and who performs well on the day of the event, enables you to be better placed to find volunteers again in future. Many successful annual events use the same volunteers year after year, which helps reduce training costs and promotes continuous improvement as people get better at performing their roles.

Training volunteers

You would not expect a paid employee to do the job without being trained – or be able to do so – so why should you expect this of a volunteer?

Given that you may be attracting volunteers on the promise of developing certain skills or responsibilities, it is perhaps even more important that you have a strong and robust training programme.

> ## ASHLEY GARLICK'S VOICE BOX
>
> As a lecturer in events management, I regularly get approached by event organisers looking for students to volunteer at their events.
>
> Most commonly it is sold as an 'opportunity to enhance their CV'.
>
> On closer inspection, I have sometimes found that the role involves standing all day on a road closure at a relatively unknown event, on a potentially cold, wet and miserable day.
>
> While this may help develop the communication and customer relations skills of a first-year student with no previous work or volunteering experience whatsoever, it is hardly surprising that it is not an attractive prospect to a final-year student who is looking for opportunities to apply advanced problem-solving and organisation skills.
>
> Merely saying that something will enhance someone's CV does not automatically make it so; it is important to think carefully about exactly what skills the role will use, and directing your recruitment to those who will want or need to develop them.

Training volunteers may be challenging, however, as volunteers are already giving up their time to help at the event and they therefore may be reluctant to give up additional time to undertake hours of training – especially if this is a one-off event.

If you have decided that there is too much training to cover on the day of the event, or an early start would make on-site training impractical, then you will have to train your volunteers in advance. This can feel like a big ask, and may mean you have to cover additional expenses – however, both you and your volunteers will feel more confident about the running of the event if important information and tasks have been covered pre-event. It also provides an opportunity to build and develop the team, who may be meeting for the first time.

If it is impractical to bring everybody together, then you could develop activities that can be completed online. This not only allows volunteers to complete some training at a time convenient to themselves, but also facilitates the storing of training records, as the completion of your online programme provides evidence of the training your volunteers have received.

Regardless of how you engage with your volunteers, you will be required to provide the appropriate training necessary for them to undertake their role. At a minimum this will include relevant health and safety training, emergency procedures and instruction on how to carry out their tasks. Additionally, you might want to develop specific skills and competencies that equip your people to do a great job, as well as instil the values of the event.

It is a good idea to also produce an information booklet that each staff member and volunteer can be given on or before the day of the event. This booklet could contain useful information which can help them respond to queries from your attendees, as well as acting as an aide-memoire of important information covered in their training. Remember, your attendees may not realise or care that the person in front of them is not a paid employee, and so will expect the same quality of service and treatment.

Managing volunteers

There is no one set way to manage volunteers on the day of an event. Each event will be different, and will require a different approach. However, there are some useful principles that can always be applied.

Many of the considerations when managing volunteers apply equally when managing employees or contractors – good management is good management.

Before the day of the event, the event organiser should have provided all working personnel with clear instructions about how to get to the site, and what to do when they arrive. This should include whether they need to get special accreditation, whether they need to come in a separate entrance and whom they should report to.

You want your volunteers to arrive in enough time to allow you to register and brief them, but not so early that they are waiting for long periods (see my next voice box). Make sure you have passed an up-to-date list of expected personnel to your front-of-house, security or accreditation team – there is nothing more demotivating (or signal of your bad planning) for staff than to arrive at an event and feel they are not wanted or expected.

For events that cover a wide geographical area, you may have instructed individuals to head straight to their designated location. In this case, it is a good idea to ensure they already have the uniform or equipment they will need, as you may not be immediately nearby to provide it.

They should also have a contact they report to on arrival, either in person or via a telephone or hand-held radio.

Keep a log of who has checked in, and follow up with those who have not. It is not unheard of for volunteers to find themselves out of contact in a signal blackspot,

ASHLEY GARLICK'S VOICE BOX

There is a phrase that is commonly used among volunteers – one that I have used myself many times – it is 'hurry up and wait'.

This phrase describes the pressure and urgency given to volunteers in getting them on-site and ready by a particular time, followed by a prolonged period of sitting around and doing nothing because there is nothing to do.

As volunteers are not paid, it is often easier for managers to set a start time long before these staff are needed. This is often to have people available 'just in case'. But, for a volunteer it can be extremely frustrating and demotivating.

Have a clear set of activities that keeps volunteers busy, even if they are not needed at that time; things like site familiarisation, role-play scenarios for training, or team-building icebreakers. These are all flexible activities that can be delivered before the formal briefing while volunteers are waiting around.

with no support or guidance from the management team. This is hugely demotivating for them, but also potentially dangerous if something were to go wrong and they were to require assistance.

Having a briefing before the event gives you the chance to welcome and thank your volunteers for giving up their time, and also to remind them of your expectations and motivate them to do a good job. At this point you should take stock of your personnel numbers, as it is quite common to have a few volunteers not show up. Whilst it could therefore be tempting to overstaff in anticipation of no-shows, you should avoid overstaffing to the point where you are sending people home at the start of the day.

Be sure to remind everyone of the process to be followed at the end of the day; if you are keeping everyone back to attend a debrief meeting, make clear where and when it will take place.

During the event, you should make sure to consider volunteer welfare. A volunteer army marches on its stomach. Adequate food and refreshments will make the difference between an enthusiastic and motivated workforce, and miserable people who just want to go home.

Remember, volunteers may not feel as beholden to your event as paid staff, not least because they do not have the fear of not getting paid at the end of the event. If you do not treat volunteers well enough, do not be surprised if they decide to pack up and go home.

Experience proves that when it comes to the day of the event, volunteers will work as hard and be just as dedicated as paid employees. If your staff are going home unexpectedly, you have done something wrong.

Events that use very large numbers of volunteers may find it challenging to manage them all, especially if the core event management team is relatively small. To tackle this issue, some events do not take on individual volunteers at all. Instead, volunteers are taken on as teams with a single nominated leader. This reduces the number of people the event team has to liaise with, as well as ensuring the teams are directly managed by someone who is familiar with the event. It is a particularly useful strategy when using local groups, clubs or societies as a source for volunteers – as they will often bring an entire team which is largely self-managed.

Legal aspects of volunteering

One of the most important legal distinctions when it comes to unpaid work is the difference between volunteering and volunteer work.

Whether someone who is not being paid is either a volunteer or volunteer worker will determine their precise legal status, protections and requirements from you as the employer.

There are many factors that can influence which category an individual would be placed in, and these will not be fully discussed here; therefore, if you remain unsure which applies, you should seek specialist advice.

In short, however, someone would usually be classed as a volunteer worker if they are bound by any contractual arrangement regarding their duties and undertakings. For example, if there is an agreement that states someone must volunteer for a certain number of hours, otherwise they would be charged a fee to pay for their training, they would likely be classed as a volunteer worker.

Regardless of whether someone is a volunteer or volunteer worker, the person for whom they undertake their service is required to check each volunteer has the legal right to do so. This usually involves checking they are legally permitted to reside and work in the country, and retaining evidence as proof these checks have taken place.

Volunteering will not normally count towards work restrictions (such as visa restrictions); however, volunteer work may do so – therefore you should seek specialist advice when using volunteer workers who are subject to any form of restriction.

While most employment legislation (in the UK) does not apply to volunteers, there is an ethical and moral question over applying standards to volunteers that would be illegal if they were paid staff. Therefore, it is good practice to treat all personnel with the same high standards.

Careful consideration should be taken, especially where the provision of certain protections might inadvertently be taken to treat the individual as a volunteer worker, rather than a volunteer. For example, if certain policies exist for volunteers which might be directly comparable to those for employees, it may make them a worker rather than a volunteer. To address this, common guidance is to either treat all staff as employees and volunteer workers, or have separate policies and procedures for paid staff and volunteers.

There is also legislation that ensures event organisers have a duty of care to both employees and volunteers. For example, the Health and Safety Act 1974 requires that as well as considering health and safety implications to employees and volunteers, the organiser would also need to consider attendees and members of the public.

Working with volunteers

Even if you are not using volunteers directly, it may be that one of your contractors, agencies or other stakeholders is. This can lead to situations where you are paying for a service, and therefore have clear expectations of the standard of service or behaviours of staff, but the individuals on-site are not receiving any of the money and therefore do not feel bound by the normal 'rules' of a transaction. For example, volunteers at a concert may use their staff access to take a vantage point at the side of the stage to watch an artist, and this may be something that you are concerned will look unprofessional. The volunteers are unlikely to know exactly what you are paying their organisation, and may not realise or have considered you are paying at all; therefore, it is normally best to discuss your concerns with a manager or senior representative of the organisation as they will have a greater understanding of the contractual relationship, rather than speaking to the volunteers themselves. It is a good idea to have discussed what is, and is not, acceptable prior to or at the start of the event; however, if a problem arises during the event, then this should be raised calmly with the contractor.

It is not uncommon for volunteers to 'try their luck', and either negotiate special access or obtain freebies such as food or merchandise. While this can be frustrating for the event organiser, it is rarely done with malicious or mal-intent. The best way to avoid any problems is to ensure all staff and contractors are briefed and trained to politely, but firmly, refuse such requests, and refer to the event management team any problems that occur.

Where there may be supplies that are surplus to requirements, you may wish to provide these to staff and volunteers. This reduces wastage that might otherwise be sent to landfill, but it can also have a hugely positive impact on relationships and generate increased levels of commitment, productivity and gratitude – as well as positive public relation (PR) for the event.

There may also be a PR company and/or a marketing company to manage such specific logistics for an event. Even so, they still report in to the event organiser at the top of the pyramidal organisational structure.

In the case of charity clients, often there is a sub-committee appointed to oversee each event and the event organiser will be reporting to that sub-committee. Committees are notorious for getting in the way of planning, which can be frustrating and result in slow decision making. But, committees do fulfil the function of ensuring the charity's goals and objectives are met with right and proper expenditure.

•   •   •

The job of event management can often be considered as being operational; that is, on-site on the day of the event. After all, that is what guests see. It is not surprising, then, that the layman attending an event thinks event management is easy and begins when the doors open and ends when the bar closes.

The reality is that the event itself is the culmination of much planning. Nothing would be there and nothing would happen if it had not been thought about, budgeted, planned, ordered, delivered, expected, checked, counted in, counted out, returned, invoiced and paid.

Guests do not need to know this. They should not even think about it. Their job is to enjoy the experience the event organiser has provided.

The unknown, hidden parts of event management begin way before the event, and end way after the event, which is why this book divides the job of event management into three parts: management pre-event; management on-site; and management post-event.

PART 2

Management pre-event

This section of this book considers every aspect of event management prior to the date of the event.

The steps and procedures are set out logically as they would occur during the planning of an event.

Chapter  4

The enquiry to confirmation stage

4.1 Enquiry

In the first instance, the event organiser will receive an event enquiry, for which an enquiry form (Appendix I) should be completed. This template prompts the event organiser to gain pertinent information about the proposed event, whilst taking the enquiry.

Failure to adhere to a standard template will allow inconsistencies and omissions of information to occur from enquiry to enquiry. The point of procedures – including administration procedures – is the consistency they provide.

The enquiry form prompts information so that the event organiser does not forget to ask any valuable question. It would be unprofessional to have to contact the potential client again and again for more information because necessary information was not garnered at the enquiry stage.

It is important to record any additional information the client offers – not only what is required on the enquiry template. It is unprofessional to reach a briefing meeting and ask questions where answers were already given at the enquiry stage but got ignored because that information was not required for the enquiry form.

The enquiry form can be treated with a degree of flexibility. If the enquiry is by telephone, for instance, perhaps not all the information will be garnered in the time frame of the call. This is why the form is designed with high-priority information at the beginning, so that it allows for partial completion and still the most necessary information will be received.

Usually, there will be an opportunity to finalise other details at a later stage if the client reacts favourably to the enquiry response.

The information provided by the prospective client may not come in the order of the form, so it is vital to listen and record any details given. The form can be tidied up later, when there is time to re-sort the information.

The enquiry form records the potential client's details from the outset. Even if the event does not actually happen, it is important to capture client data for future marketing purposes. Building an enquiry database enables the event organiser to pursue previous potential clients to offer promotions, discounts, notifications and invitations to showcase evenings. It may also be relevant to contact the enquirer in good time for planning next year's event if it was an enquiry for an annual occasion, such as a Christmas party.

It must become habit to complete an enquiry form for every enquiry, even those that are certain not to happen – if the venue is too small for the event, for instance. The forms will help gauge the level of enquiries over a period so as to measure busy and slack times. This enables marketing initiatives or promotions to be planned and implemented.

It is also important to record from where each enquiry was generated – the source – so as to measure the effectiveness of websites, the various social media platforms, and advertising or marketing campaigns.

4.2 Brief

Every event begins with an idea or a need and there is always an objective.

Whomever decides these, also needs to **brief** them to the person organising the event.

After receiving the enquiry, the event organiser is responsible for correctly *taking the brief*.

When the brief takes place can vary.

If the client is a first-time client, the relationship with the event organiser is untested. In this case, the client will expect a proposal from the event organiser, and if the proposal is agreeable, the event organiser will be invited to take the event brief to firm up the details and costs.

If the client is a repeat client and the relationship with the event organiser is trusted, the client may call the event organiser in to receive the brief without the need for a proposal to be submitted beforehand.

It is important here to recognise that an enquiry response is not the same as a proposal because an enquiry response can be fulfilled with the limited information on the enquiry form. This may include generic details such as venue hire costs and sample menus with menu costs. Whereas the detailed information and event requirements necessary to write a proposal are garnered from the brief.

The brief is about the exchange of information. It is a communication.

But, the client may not know what to brief the event organiser on. Maybe the client is inexperienced in events and only thinks or believes they know. Or, the

AUTHOR'S VOICE BOX

Wherever possible, I try to take the brief at the client's office, rather than meeting at a hotel, the venue or in my office.

I know where I work and what it looks like, so it tells me nothing about the environment in which my client works. Meetings in hotels can be a nice experience, but again I learn little about how my client works.

Seeing the client's working environment allows me to gauge their professionalism and the culture they work within: is it tidy, organised, smart, technical, modern . . . ?

Subtle clues provide a foundation from which to develop the client relationship: do they have a wonderful view of the city? This can be a starting point for conversation. And, it enables the continuation of discussion wherever I next meet the client.

In a client's office there is always something to identify their personality and lifestyle, too. They may smoke; they may have a picture of their dog on the desk; they may collect porcelain pigs! I want to know these things, and I want to discover if we have things in common. I have a dog, for example. I do not collect porcelain pigs, but I could always purchase one as a gift for the client.

At later stages of the event process, it will be easier and more logical to conduct meetings at the chosen venue or at a midway point. So, it is good practice to travel to the client's office sooner rather than later.

client could be experienced in events, but even then, not as widely experienced as an event organiser.

So, the event organiser must be in the position of steering and guiding the client, even at this early stage. It is not for the client to lead the event organiser. It can be important to establish the relationship at this earliest opportunity.

When taking the brief, the event organiser is provided with the first opportunity to demonstrate authority, experience, knowledge, professionalism and creativity.

At the briefing meeting, the client is not *telling* the event organiser how the event must be done. Rather, the client is *asking* how their requirements can be achieved. The client should impart what is wanted for their event, and it is expected that the event organiser should propose how to achieve it.

The event organiser's advice and experience are key to the formula of success. This is why the client placed the enquiry and is not managing the event themselves.

However, not all clients understand this relationship, so it can be a delicate act of persuasion and coercion before the client empowers the event organiser to make decisions, suggest alternatives and get on with the job of event management.

Questions are essential for the event organiser to obtain as much information as possible at the brief.

Every snippet of information is vital. The importance of this will become evident when building the proposal of ideas and forming the budget. After all, it would be unprofessional to email the client with every little question that occurs during construction of the proposal.

4.2.1 Briefing template

When invited to take an event brief, the experienced event organiser will know the usual questions to ask:

- date of the event
- location of the event
- type and style of venue
- number of guests
- the reason for the event
- style of catering

- budget
- itinerary.

Even so, it is prudent to have a briefing template for questions that one may otherwise forget to ask.

Some event organisers take a standard questionnaire along to briefing meetings, with questions such as the names of VIPs attending; whether there will be invitations and, if so, who is to print them; what catering style is preferred; will press be allowed inside the venue; and so on. Then, they fill in the answers as the briefing meeting progresses.

4.3 Proposal

After the brief has been taken, the research begins.

It starts with researching the date of the event. Does the date clash with anything happening on a local level that would compete for guests' attendance, their time and interest, or the interest of the media?

It is important to also research the date on a national and international level, too.

The launch of a new product will not make forward-page news if it launches on the same day as a royal wedding, for example.

The proposal is built on the foundation of research and the budget is woven into the walls.

The ease of research will depend on the quality of the brief and, to some degree, the complexity of the event.

Sometimes, though, the client is not forthcoming with information – maybe because they do not have details at the time of the brief.

Often, a client will expect the event organiser to submit information, creative ideas, logistical solutions and the costs in the proposal as a kind of test of their expertise and professionalism.

Sometimes, a client will ask for an event proposal solely to garner creative ideas and then they might suggest them to another event organiser who is pitching for the job but is cheaper, has a better rapport with the client or is already known to them.

Or, the client may take the proposition that was presented and then organise the event themselves and with their own staff now that they have new ideas.

In some cases, a client may simply wish to explore how much it would cost to put on an event, without fully intending to commit.

These pitfalls with new clients are difficult to avoid because the event proposal must be honest and realistic. This is one hazard of the job. The only way to avoid unscrupulous clients is by having repeat clients with whom you develop a relationship and trust.

Providing a proposal to a client is not obligatory. Event organisers have been known to take a brief, but decline to submit a proposal without first receiving a commitment to be contracted for the job. Or, if the chemistry between the client and the event organiser is not healthy even at this stage, the event organiser should not want the job anyway. It may not be good business practice, but neither is a bad event.

Attempts can be made to overcome these pitfalls by pitching for a job. Most proposals carry statements of 'copyright', or other worded caveats such as 'all creative ideas belong to Berners Events Ltd'. But, these are mere deterrents without much substance, as in most instances it would not be known that the client went ahead with an idea, and what could be done about it if they had? It would also be difficult to prove nobody else had the same idea.

4.3.1 Pitching

Pitching the proposal – or being invited to *pitch* for an event – means the client is openly inviting other event organisers to pitch for winning the same job. Because of the element of competition for the job, pitching is a little more aggressive than merely submitting an excellent proposal.

Often, it will mean attending the client's offices to present the proposal in a creative and exciting fashion.

Sometimes, the client will require proposals to be submitted in written form as the first step in the process of deciding which event organisers will subsequently be invited to pitch.

The elements incorporated in the proposal are outlined in subsequent chapters.

4.4 Budget proposal

Usually, a client will not reveal the budget at the briefing stage. It is lucky if they do, but this seems to be a matter of trust. If it is a regular client for the event organiser, the client will most likely share the budget details at the outset – the enquiry stage.

Not knowing the budget from the outset is frustrating because the event organiser is forced to prepare the proposal and budget without knowing how much the client wishes to spend on the event.

It is not unusual for a client to receive a carefully prepared proposal and then declare it as being too expensive and *this* is when the event organiser finally learns how much the client wishes to spend. It would be so much easier the other way around, but this is not how clients work. If it *is* a trust thing, the client will be unwilling to reveal how much is in their pot, and will wait to see how much the event organiser proposes it will cost.

Or, the client will wait to read the proposal and then ask for the costs to be reduced by a certain amount, which would have been beneficial to have known before sitting down to write the proposal.

Some costs will be easy to calculate, such as the venue hire fee, the hire of furniture, and the event organiser's management fee – which is usually a percentage of between 12.5% and 15% of the total event budget. Not always is the management fee a percentage of total budget: it can be charged as a flat fee or as a minimum fee.

Other costs are more difficult to determine, and these usually relate to the creativity of the event, or are elements dependent upon the number of guests or delegates – such as catering, bar spend, and the cost of delegate packs. So, the event organiser who is writing the proposal is working blind with their ideas until the client either approves the spend or asks for elements to be trimmed so as to reduce the budget.

There are, however, other means for an event organiser to achieve income.

4.4.1 Mark-up

Mark-up is where the event organiser charges the client more than the cost of an item.

So, if the hire of 500 chairs costs £500, the event organiser may charge the client £600 and earn a £100 mark-up on the transaction.

The practice of mark-up is legitimate, legal and widespread – we all pay mark-up whenever we buy something in a shop. We expect the shopkeeper to earn a profit from the mark-up. Yet, event clients consider mark-up to be greedy and unscrupulous. They expect to see all costs with transparency presented in the budget. And, if the event organiser's profit is through the management fee, a client would not expect to shell out for the event organiser to achieve hidden additional profit.

The risk is that the client can find out how much it costs to hire 500 chairs and then refer to how much they have been charged by their event organiser, who may already be receiving a management fee. So, there is a 'lie' involved even though shops buy in items for less than they sell them for, which is pure mark-up.

An event organiser can lose clients through mark-up – and lost clients talk to potential clients, so reputation is at stake.

4.4.2 Commission

Another source of revenue for the event organiser is commission. If 500 chairs cost £500 to hire, the event organiser may receive £50 back for the business they provide to that chair supplier. It can be seen as a loyalty payment.

The arrangement between the event organiser and the supplier may be per event or over a year's worth of business transactions.

Commission encourages event organisers to be loyal to their suppliers – especially in competitive services, such as catering and furniture hire.

Sometimes, an event organiser will have a 'deal' with a venue and will receive commission for placing clients there.

An event organiser receiving commission from suppliers appears to be more acceptable to clients than mark-up, even though the saving could be passed on to the client. Certainly, commission is less risky for the client to discover.

The client may not be pleased to learn of these practices that generate additional income for the event organiser. Most clients expect the budget to be spent on the event, and any savings would allow for additional items such as more drinks. But, mark-up, commission and supplier discounts ensure the event organiser is not relying solely on the management fee for their income.

4.4.3 Contingency

If the brief is detailed and the specifics of costs are known, such as 500 wristbands are required, these costs are easily ascertained and built into the budget.

Many costs are variable, however, and largely depend on the number of guests attending. And, other costs may be hidden or unexpected. So it is wise to build a contingency into the budget if there is room to do so.

Contingency is often viewed as a failsafe for when things go wrong. This can be dangerous because it can get overlooked, or a confident event organiser may feel they do not need to budget for 'things going wrong'.

So, contingency should be treated as a cushion for additional expenditure. Clients are wont to add elements later on, or think of something new. Or, they may have assumed an element was included, so did not ask for it.

If the contingency is not used, it can be returned to the client because nothing additional was required. It is better than returning it because 'nothing went wrong'.

It is worth noting here that a bar spend is always a hazardous element to calculate in advance. Whatever is budgeted for alcohol will almost always be not enough. It is helpful to have some leeway in the budget, which the contingency may mop up.

If the event enquiry is from a new client, the decision to award the job will largely come down to cost. Well, the client has asked you to submit a proposal, so they already know your reputation or your portfolio.

Because of cost, a client will often scan past the carefully submitted ideas and venue proposals, only for their eye to settle on the summary line of the budget.

It is a good idea, therefore, to set the budget out as a 'shopping list', so that the client can choose to include or preclude elements based on cost. This also allows the client to get involved with the decision-making process. They can see what they are getting for their money and may even decide to up the budget if they like everything that has been proposed.

Not always is the decision down to money. The client's personal and professional reputation is at stake, and so is the reputation of the client organisation. The last thing needed is public embarrassment if guests do not enjoy the event or something – anything – is unprofessional. The client's reputation for efficiency in their job will be tarnished. Certainly, if the guests are clients of the organisation, a poor event will do serious harm.

So, rather than setting himself up as an event organiser who does cheap events – which in itself is not a good idea – an event organiser should be aware of other factors that can sway a client: events in the event organiser's portfolio, testimonials from previous clients, professionalism, experience and the personal chemistry from the outset.

The successful event organiser must keep in mind that business is won by relationships.

People don't like doing business with people they don't like.

A client may brief two or three event organisers or event management companies. If this is the case, the factors mentioned previously become the real difference between winning a job and losing it.

4.5 Confirmation

If the proposal is accepted by the client (or the pitch is won), the client should send a confirmation to the event organiser. Each event organiser works differently, so the confirmation could be accepted by email, letter, telephone or in person.

Often, the client and event organiser will meet to discuss the proposal and work through adjustments. Adjustments may be due to the client's preferences, the style of the event or trimming elements in the proposal to fit the budget.

Most event organisers will raise a contract for the client to sign when confirmation is received.

A contract should protect both parties. Unforeseen circumstances do arise and even long-term relationships can change. Things do go wrong. Financial situations and certainties alter. Cancellations happen.

Importantly, event management is a competitive industry and a client may be tempted to try another event organiser if a contract is not in place to prevent them from so doing.

Chapter **5**

Management of the lead-in

5.1 Lead-in

The lead-in is the distance between receiving the confirmation and the date of the event.

The work of planning the event truly begins once confirmation is received and the job is no longer speculative. It can be seen, therefore, how important it is to submit a proposal in good time and receive the confirmation from the client as quickly as possible because these impact on the amount of lead-in.

If it is not already known from the enquiry, the first question at the briefing meeting is always to ascertain the date of the event. Thus, the event organiser will know how much lead-in there is.

If it is a short lead-in and the event is complex or technical, some event organisers are likely to decline the job. This may seem bad business, but it is also bad business to rush into an event with not enough time, and end up with a failure. A good lead-in is essential – and a good client will know this.

Before the event happens there will be much research, organising, a venue to source and book, elements to be sourced and hired, discussions with suppliers and negotiations with contractors, and invitations will need to be sent well in advance and responses received.

A short lead-in has a severe negative impact upon choices and decision making: the availability of venues will get limited; the availability of trusted suppliers may be compromised which means procuring elements from unknown sources; preparatory tasks, such as printing or set design, may end up getting rushed.

A short or tight lead-in should act as an alarm bell for an event organiser. After all, why is the lead-in short? The client would surely have known that the event was happening. Or, was it a last-minute thing with no strategy and has it not been fully thought through? It may just be down to bad planning or poor organisation by the client, which signals this is the way it will run. In other words, this is the culture of the organisation or the level of unprofessionalism typical of it. This can have implications for the event organiser, such as late payments or downsizing the budget at a later stage.

Otherwise, it could be that the tight lead-in is due to a previous event organiser being fired or having resigned. This possibility should be investigated and the causes understood before rushing in to pick up a last-minute job.

A short lead-in tends to result in quick decisions, late action, rash solutions and unsatisfactory results.

AUTHOR'S VOICE BOX

Another issue I have with short lead-ins is that I like to begin working on a project from the very beginning.

I do not want to win an event job and find that the venue is already booked – and not by me. It means I have to build a client/venue relationship without having been involved in their discussions and negotiations. Or, the venue may not be the one I would have chosen because of its standards or suitability.

It is the same with other elements – the caterers, for example. Maybe I have worked with them before and would not recommend them.

If decided for me, these elements are out of my control before I have even started doing my job.

Event management is not about managing unsatisfactory results. It is about forward planning.

Forward planning is proactive management – it happens beforehand.

A short lead-in forces *reactive* management where decisions are made too late or as a result of being short of time.

There are times when a short lead-in is legitimate – the need to hastily arrange a press conference or a political speech, for example. In which case, the event organiser should have experience of staging events at short notice. What is important is the known ability to provide an exemplary event within the time frame.

The question is: what determines a good or a short lead-in?

It depends largely upon the complexity of the event. Which is why the answer changes for each event.

The more elements there are to organise and plan, the more time is needed.

However, this is not a solid rule. Conferences in a conference centre could be viewed as not very complex. But, the need to book keynote speakers, call for papers, promote the conference to the marketplace and process delegate registrations, all in good time for people's diaries, requires a lengthy lead-in.

AUTHOR'S VOICE BOX

As a rule set by myself, my minimum lead-in for an event is three months.

If I receive an enquiry and the date of the event is under three months away, I am likely to decline the job. Experience has taught me not to accept last-minute jobs.

Rules can be broken, though. If it is a straightforward event, such as a canapé reception, and I know the client already and am familiar with the venue I am using, then I will be flexible.

The key point to remember with lead-in times is to assess the risk of the event not being well planned, because there was not enough time to do the planning.

AUTHOR'S VOICE BOX

From another viewpoint of lead-in times, I once worked on an annual golf event that took place on the Algarve.

Each year, the event organiser got busy with organising other events and so she allowed nine months to elapse until time forced her to think about the approaching golf event.

That meant she was only reacquainting herself with the previous year's sponsors nine months after the tournament and with only three months until the next tournament. It was a case of dusting off her hands when the event was over, and only thinking about it again when it crept close in her diary.

When I became involved with the event, I changed the timeline so that instead of a nine-month downtime, the event had a nine-month lead-in.

Just that change means that the sponsors were approached quickly at the close of the event when they were still basking in the glow of participating in a successful event in the fabulous Algarve sunshine – what better way to get them to commit their sponsorship for next time?

It also meant that the sponsorship funding got secured in good time so that the budget could be planned well in advance. And, it allowed the event organiser to liaise with the sponsors for most of the year so she could develop ongoing relationships with them, rather than leaving them for nine months by which time they may even have moved on.

This demonstrates how lead-in times can be manipulated so that they work for, and not against, the event organiser.

5.2 The venue

The venue for the event is a key factor and most elements of an event rest on the size, location, restrictions and cost of the venue.

Therefore, not much else can be planned without the venue being known.

Not only is the hire of a venue likely to be one of the costliest elements in the budget, but the style, quality and on-site facilities at the venue determine how many elements need to be hired in. This impacts logistics, planning and costs.

In most cases, the proposal of venues at this earliest stage of organising an event requires basic research and merely suggests to the client the cost and availability of potential venues.

But, if it is a repeat client or the job is confirmed, the venue search will be of such importance that not much else can be achieved without knowing which venue is being used to host the event.

Venue searching is so critical and the research so demanding that it has become a stand-alone sector of the events industry. There are venue-sourcing companies, agencies, freelancers and location scouts.

Television and film production companies employ location scouts to find places that suit filming purposes. Or, they use location search agencies, as do PR and marketing companies when searching for locations for their clients' marketing videos, television advertisements or photo-shoots.

Event organisers also use location finders for placing their clients' events into unusual venues that otherwise are not known or not available to hire. Fashion shows, parties, launches and many other types of event require location searches, as well as venue searches.

Unusual venues should make themselves known to event organisers, location search companies, location scouts, location agents, film production companies, and marketing and PR companies.

AUTHOR'S VOICE BOX

I received a brief from a record label wanting to stage a live rock band performance on a beach in Italy.

The starting point of writing the proposal meant my having to visit Naples, Sorrento, Ravello, Positano and Amalfi to scout beachside venues.

The venue search is an event in itself.

For this project, the client awarded me a separate budget to scout for venues.

When the client authorised the scouting trip, the proposal was not the utmost priority, but finding the right venue. In other words, without the venue there was no proposal.

It is not only venues that are required for locations. Film producers and event organisers often search for historic houses, mansions, warehouses, high-tech office developments, derelict houses, disused buildings, car parks, shopping centres, scenic vistas, beaches, period houses and buildings with interesting architecture.

Demand is driven by clients who are increasingly demanding exciting and unusual venues to highlight their event, outdo their competitors or improve on the previous year's event.

Even straightforward parties, such as an office Christmas party, have to better the party that the guests experienced last year.

No longer are hotels perceived as good enough for staging events. In fact, clients often frown upon the idea of staging their event in a hotel because hotels are not considered to be creative environments for events. Hotels have acquired a reputation for being staid and boring. Hotels are considered unimaginative, easy and lazy. With some exceptions, of course, hotel ballrooms and function suites are not renowned for their imaginative décor.

Nevertheless, hotels are still busy event venues because they offer a one-stop shop for regular events, such as dinners, balls and, of course, conferences. All facilities are in situ, including technical equipment, catering, bars, cloakrooms, toilets, staff, management and, naturally, accommodation if this is one of the requirements of the event. It would not be unfair to say that the true value of holding events in hotels comes from the requirement of bedrooms.

Unfortunately for hotels, the one-stop shop concept has become synonymous with having a limited budget. It means nothing need be hired in because it is already there at the hotel. This reduces costs. This is how the perception evolved that if the client holds their event in a one-stop shop – a hotel – they must have a low budget. This brings us back to why many clients instruct their event organiser to avoid hotels.

Hotels may also be avoided by event organisers themselves because of the abundance of in-house facilities. One may be forgiven for thinking in-situ facilities would be an advantage in terms of logistics, timings and cost. But, for an event organiser, event company or production company the add-ons they bring in to a venue are opportunities to increase their income by commission or mark-up from additional items. If the hotel provides everything, there is little room for the event organiser to increase revenue.

Many event clients need their event to be noticed. And, they want it to be remembered. Events are staged in underground car parks and multi-storey car parks; in Windsor Great Park and London's Hyde Park; in nightclubs, warehouses, offices, country estates, castles, derelict buildings and Park Lane hotels. Events happen everywhere.

AUTHOR'S VOICE BOX

One event organiser's office in central London has vast bookshelves laden with brochures from venues all over the UK.

Even though most research is carried out online, building a library of venues is helpful to jog the memory, and have pictures and specifications to hand.

Writing event proposals requires instant access to venues that are suitable for the event. Otherwise, it lengthens the time required to search for venues.

A library of venue brochures helps to quickly preclude venues that are unsuitable on the basis of elements like a lack of space or low ceiling height.

The most valuable use of time at the research stage – which is when the job may not even be confirmed yet – is to quickly eliminate venues that would not work for the event. After all, this is working for free!

It is this exposure of events that has led to students wanting to learn about the business of organising events, whereas once upon a time events were an offshoot of the hotel industry.

There are many sources for finding venues. Town halls and tourist offices often stock brochures of venues in the locality and can be a good place to start if looking for a venue in an unfamiliar location.

In developed markets venues exist side by side in an extremely competitive environment and are keen to win event business – even if events are not their core business, such as museums and art galleries. In such markets there are printed and online venue directories to assist the event organiser with finding a venue. Also, there are event trade exhibitions, such as International Confex, which showcase venues and event services.

In addition, there are specialist event-finding agencies that may not organise events, but do match organisers with venues. Sometimes, these agencies masquerade as simply event-finding companies, but are a front for other event services such as catering. A word of caution here for the event organiser: be aware of 'event-finding agencies' that actually *do* organise events, because you may unwittingly provide them with an enquiry for a potential client who is not yet contracted with yourself.

Venue-finding agencies may charge a finding fee, which will be in addition to the hire fee that the venue will charge. The finding fee can be worthwhile if the event organiser does not have the time or resources to find a venue themselves.

Sometimes the venue-finding agent receives commission directly from the venue. There is need for another note of caution here: venue-finding agencies are sales-oriented, so they may recommend venues based on the level of their reward, rather than the quality of the venue or its suitability for the event.

Finding the right venue can be straightforward, quick and easy. Or, it can be complicated, hard work and time-consuming. The difference is usually down to the event organiser's knowledge of the target location.

Sometimes an enquiry will be received and the event organiser will immediately know where to place it because the location is familiar, or because the venue has been used before and would again be suitable for the new event. This is often the case with standard events such as weddings and Christmas parties.

Other times it will take three weeks of painful research, phone calls and urgent requests for brochures to be sent from venues.

For all events – without exception – the event organiser has to *recce* (short for reconnaissance or reconnoitre) the suitability of venues. But, when organising an event in a distant location or another country, foreign consultants (*ground agents*) provide invaluable help at this stage. It is they who will do the recce in your distant absence. Not only can they personally recommend venues from their local knowledge and experience, but they can conduct ongoing research in the event organiser's absence during the event planning stages.

The services of foreign consultants may extend further than finding a venue. A ground agent can source all local requirements for the event – from taxi companies to security, and from florists to caterers. It also helps because they speak the language and understand the culture.

Caution is to be advised when contracting foreign consultants, however. The event organiser will be at the consultant's mercy. The consultant will know the people, the locations and the language (so in this instance becomes the 'real' event organiser). So if there should be a breakdown in the relationship between the event organiser and the ground agent, it can be assured that every local supplier will side with the consultant.

Without using tourist guidebooks, venue directories, venue-finding agencies or foreign consultants, and if the event organiser's knowledge of venues in the locality is not excellent, the only way to find a venue is by footwork.

AUTHOR'S VOICE BOX

For a VIP event in southern Europe, I researched two ground agents and placed the enquiry with each.

But, one consultant cleverly reserved all the private-hire limousines and private security companies as soon as I gave her the date of the event.

I had no choice but to place the contract with her and not the other ground agent, otherwise I would have had no limousines and security for the event.

And, I only discovered this because the second ground agent began his job and found that most of what was required had already been reserved.

Event organisers are location scouts and often feel the need to walk round a city and visit the public buildings, such as libraries, theatres, art galleries and museums, to see if any are suitable to accommodate events.

If there is a choice of available venues at the location, the event organiser may propose two or three venues to the client, and take the client to view the proposed venues (this is known as a *venue show-round*. See 5.2.1). This is a way of involving the client in the decision process so that the client can make their choice from the venues which the event organiser has already deemed suitable. This is expected behaviour in cities where the proposed venues are abundant and close by, and it is important because the client should be involved in the key element of venue choice.

AUTHOR'S VOICE BOX

Whereas it is common for event organisers to show two or three venues to their client, I try to recommend just one venue before taking the client to see it and approve my choice.

I would have eliminated a range of venues during my research, and will point out the reasons why, just so that my client feels assured that I have done the research on their behalf and, based upon my experience, I have arrived at the best venue for their event.

What I am attempting to achieve is for the client to agree with *my* choice of venue for their event.

5.2.1 Venue show-round

When taking a client on a tour of shortlisted venues, the event organiser should have already ensured that each venue is suitable for the event requirements, and is available on the date of the event.

If logistically possible, the proposed venues should be visited by the event organiser in advance of the client show-round so as to brief the venue manager and begin the working relationship. It will also help to view the facilities and arrange how they will be presented to the client during the client show-round. This groundwork also ensures that the event organiser knows how to find the venue and how to gain access – which door to use, which bell to press, whom to ask for and so on.

The event organiser's good relationship with the venue is all-important. So, if the event organiser happens to clash with the venue management for some reason, it is better for this to occur at a visit when the client is not present.

Many venues consider the event organiser to be the go-between, and treat them with an informal camaraderie – an 'in the trade' approach that borders on

---

AUTHOR'S VOICE BOX

I took a client to view a very exclusive celebrity haunt in London's West End. Its celebrity clientele perhaps caused me to assume the venue was professional. Reflecting on this, I realise celebrities do not hang out at venues because of the professionalism.

Anyhow, my client show-round was booked for 10:30 am, but the venue was still in a state of recovery from the revelry of the night before. Glasses and empty bottles were everywhere; the floor was littered; the rooms stank of alcohol . . .

It was a poor reflection of the notable venue and I was embarrassed to take my client to view the venue I had recommended.

I was disappointed that the venue manager had agreed to schedule the visit at that time of the morning despite knowing it took his cleaning team so long to recover the venue, and I thought it unprofessional of him to expose his venue in such a poor state.

But, he taught me the rule to never take a client to view a venue before midday.

unprofessionalism. However, whereas a client may represent a one-off booking for the venue, the event organiser creates events for a living and can provide ongoing business to the venue. So, it is wise to maintain a professional stance with all contractors and suppliers, including the venue.

Hotels appear to systematically add all clients to their database and will direct-approach. This is probably due to the sales-led nature of the hotel business. Many event organisers avoid placing events into hotels for this reason.

The venue show-round is an event itself – it could be referred to as a 'pre-event'.

From a venue management point of view, the venue should be ready to welcome the prospective client 15 minutes before the scheduled arrival time. This is professional and courteous. Coffee should be awaiting the client's arrival.

The venue should be well-presented, clean and fresh. All facilities and rooms should be available for viewing and not occupied by an ongoing event or conference. If the nature of the prospective event is known – a conference, say – the venue should be presented in a conference setting with conference lighting.

All venue staff must be made aware of a scheduled client visit so that they are not lazing around or swearing, as staff and crew are wont to do.

AUTHOR'S VOICE BOX

I once took a client on a show-round of an expensive venue in central London and witnessed the venue manager exchange business cards with my client.

Later that week, my client contacted me to let me know the venue manager had offered their in-house event management expertise over mine.

Theirs was a short-sighted business ethic that would make more enemies than friends in an industry that survives on good reputation. I never took business to that venue again.

Many event organisers are nervous of such practice and will ask the venue manager not to exchange business cards with the client. This is difficult to impose, so I would rather build my client relations so they will always want me to organise their events and would not risk placing their business with other organisers or venue managers.

Background music should be playing to lessen the formality of the atmosphere and to encourage relations to develop between the client and event organiser, and the event organiser and venue.

For a straightforward event, the event organiser may visit the venue two or three times during pre-event planning – the lead-in time. This may or may not be with the client attending, but will be to finalise menus, delivery schedules, location of bars and seating arrangements, and to run through the details with various departments, such as caterers, technicians and security.

More complex events may necessitate five, six or more visits to the venue. The more suppliers, entertainers, contractors and other outsourced requirements there are, the more meetings will be required, as each will need at least one meeting to be held at the venue to 'walk through' their role. Nothing is left to chance.

5.2.1.1 Venue limitations

Another reason for the venue being the starting point of the proposal is that the venue dictates what can and cannot be achieved.

Often, there exist venue restrictions and limitations, which may include the following.

* Low ceiling height

For creativity to happen in events, height is required for balloon nets, confetti cannons, indoor pyrotechnics, special effect lighting and projection.

In many venues – particularly hotels – there is not enough room height to suspend a projector, hang lights or erect a screen.

The higher the budget, the higher the ceiling!

* Restricted access

The venue may be perfect for the event, except that the scenery will not fit through the doors, or deliveries can only take place during specified hours, or the venue has to close to the public before private access is permitted.

Accessing a car into a venue with steps or narrow doorways is one to watch for here.

* The venue is too small

It makes sense not to book a venue that is too small to accommodate the guests, stage, tables and chairs, and all other elements required.

A venue's capacity is a legal obligation to prevent overcrowding or problems with emergency evacuation. Management, staff and crew are included in a venue's legal capacity.

- The venue is too large

This is not so obvious as the previous point. But, it is also a problem to book a venue which is too big. There is nothing worse than a few hundred people milling around in a venue that can accommodate a few thousand – it will look as if nobody bothered to turn up.

It is always preferable for a venue to be on the smaller side – especially if it is a launch event or a party. This way, it looks as if the event is popular and well-attended.

- Restricted sightlines

The venue may seem perfect for the event until somebody points out that the view of the stage is obstructed by pillars or columns.

High balconies with ceilings are also a common feature which restricts the audience from seeing everything happening on stage.

When selecting a venue, think of the position of the stage and plan the seating arrangements to ensure everybody in the audience can see.

Often, a venue will provide standard seating plans that will show how many seats have unrestricted and restricted views of the stage.

Consider also that all guests must be able to *hear* what is happening on stage, as well as see it.

- Bars

Bars are busy places, so ensure there are enough bars and they are located in suitable areas for the flow of guests at your event.

Even if the venue has fixed bars, they may not always be suitable for the style of event – if guests will be arriving at one time, or delegates will be breaking from a meeting and hitting the bars all at once. If necessary, install extra satellite bars to cope with demand.

- Cloakroom

Is there a cloakroom? Is it large enough? Is it visible and easy to find? Check that it is not located too near the busy entrance area where crowding and queuing can occur. Too many times, entrances and exits get blocked by the cloakroom queue.

Another frequent irritant is having the cloakroom queue snaking outside the venue because the cloakroom is located just inside the front doors.

- Toilets

Check there are plenty of toilet facilities for the number and demographic of guests. This is a legal requirement.

- Guest arrival and departure

Consider parking facilities. Where are guests having to park and walk from if it is raining? Will guests be walking over the lawn or through the mud? Maybe a covered walkway is required.

What about guests leaving the event in the dark hours? Exterior lighting needs to be hired.

- Red wine

Be cautious when hiring historic buildings. Many such venues do not allow red wine to be served because it stains carpets and white marble flooring.

AUTHOR'S VOICE BOX

At Tina Turner's summer open-air concert at Woburn Abbey there were 60,000 guests.

They arrived in glorious summer sunshine and were directed to park their cars in neat rows on the surrounding fields.

After the concert, darkness had descended and 60,000 people were wandering the unlit fields of a country estate in an attempt to find their cars in total darkness.

A great concert, yes; but it took three hours for guests to exit the venue and *that's* what they'll remember!

Some venues do not allow brown food to be served and may insist on seated dining, not buffets or canapés where food is more easily dropped onto carpets and floors.

• • •

For all the potential failings that may present themselves when sourcing a venue, identifying the restrictions and limitations is helpful to eliminate venues from the search. It would be poor management to propose a venue to a client and discover at a later stage that there are limitations and restrictions that will impede the creativity of the event.

Problems with venues occur only when the wrong venue was chosen and it is unsuitable. Or, where there was no choice available.

There are occasions when the venue cannot be proposed by the event organiser. This may be because the client has already chosen the venue or has booked it. Or, the event is held there every year. Or, it is the only venue in the locality.

In circumstances such as these, the event organiser must work with what is presented, and will need to adjust the event to suit the venue. As long as the event organiser is prepared and there is enough lead-in time, solutions can be implemented during the planning stages.

One of the key indicators to identify whether a venue is suitable for an event, is whether it has previously hosted events of the same or a similar nature. Even unusual venues may have prior experience of weddings, say. This will also indicate the level of experience of the management and staff at a venue.

5.2.1.2 Unusual venues

Built-for-purpose venues – such as conference halls for conferences and hotels for banquets – provide all the facilities required for that type of event. This is why events were always held in dedicated venues. However, clients are looking to impress their guests and outdo their competitors, which is why *unusual venues* are increasingly being sought.

Unusual venues include country houses, castles, warehouses, museums, art galleries, historic houses and landmarks.

One vital difference between a dedicated venue and an unusual venue is the experience of the venue and its staff in hosting events.

It stands to reason that a conference centre would have good experience of hosting conferences. They will have practised procedures that are tried and tested, and make the job of the event organiser easier, quicker and exposed to less risk. Even so, one conference centre may offer different standards of service from another.

Unusual venues may not have such practised procedures and experience. Even if the unusual venue is promoting itself as a venue that hosts events, and has a boastful portfolio of previous clients, this is no guarantee of their event management professionalism or skills.

Many unusual venues have diversified their offering to capture new markets. Their core business is not events. Therefore, they may not have management and staff who are trained in the art of events management, and it could be that the way they do events is *their* way of doing events.

5.2.1.3 Green-field venues

The most complex venue is a *green-field* site where nothing exists and all requirements must be hired in. This type of event necessitates a high budget, a very experienced event organiser and detailed planning. Detailed planning requires a good lead-in time, remember.

Disused warehouses, ruined buildings, car parks and marquee sites are green-field sites as well, but can sometimes be referred to as *brown-field* sites because there is a certain amount of infrastructure on-site.

AUTHOR'S VOICE BOX

I was asked to organise a celebration in a green-field site – a public garden.

There were many restrictions, such as being open to the public during the build, restrictions with serving alcohol, no damage to the plants and no vehicles on grassed areas.

The build was from scratch and required marquees, mobile toilets, catering tents, kitchens, fittings, furniture, carpets and chandeliers.

It seemed they wanted me to perform magic. But, all I could provide was the height of logistical planning.

It took time to plan in meticulous detail around the restrictions of the venue. And, it required trusted suppliers whom I could rely upon to work within the restrictions and protect my reputation with this client.

5.2.1.4 Venue deposit

Once the venue has been proposed, viewed and agreed on, it is usual for the venue to raise a contract for the event organiser or client to sign.

The venue will require the deposit to secure the date.

The deposit is usually the full amount of the *venue hire fee* (see 5.2.1.6), although some venues accept a partial hire fee as the deposit with the balance being paid at a determined date.

If the event gets cancelled, the deposit may not be returnable. Or, it may be returnable in part, which is determined by a scale of how long in advance of the event date notice of cancellation was received. So, if the event is cancelled three months before the event date, a full refund may be due. Whereas if the event gets cancelled three weeks before the event date, no refund may be given (see 5.2.1.7).

The venue deposit payment will be drawn from the event budget provided by the client. It is not expected for the event organiser to make any outlay. At this stage, the budget may not be available to the event organiser, even though the event organiser may feel pressured by the venue to pay the deposit and secure the venue so as not to lose it to another booking. Even so, the event organiser should not outlay the venue deposit.

The event organiser must never consider a venue is booked until the deposit is paid and the booking contract is signed.

Similarly, a venue can never consider an event booking as confirmed until the deposit has been received and the booking contract signed by the client or the event organiser as the client's representative.

5.2.1.5 Provisional hold

A venue will hold the date of the event on a provisional basis without charge whilst the event organiser liaises with the client, submits a proposal (which includes proposed venues that are on provisional hold because this lessens the risk of losing venues during the proposal process) and arranges a client show-round to decide the venue.

Provisionally holding a venue will prevent it being sold to another enquiry on the same date and allows the event organiser to proceed with confidence that the venues being proposed to the client are being held.

It is helpful and more manageable to agree a date with the venue when the provisional hold expires.

At some point, the event organiser will need to either release the provisional hold or confirm the booking.

The venue may chase the event organiser to get the enquiry confirmed – particularly if another enquiry is received for the same date. But, the event organiser cannot rely on the venue to get in contact, which is why an expiry date should be agreed.

Some venues will entertain other enquiries for the same date without informing the first enquiry. Or, the period of provisional hold may have expired and the venue may not have reminded the first enquiry. It is crucial for the event organiser to keep the venue updated and extend the provisional hold if necessary.

Venues are concerned with selling their space. It does not matter to them who buys it. So, the priorities of the venue and the event organiser are not always aligned.

Venue management is a yield management business. Thus, provisional hold arrangements largely depend on the relationship and close communication between the event organiser and the venue.

5.2.1.6 Venue hire fee

The hire fee (*facility fee*) is the cost for using the premises.

Some venues include other items within their hire fee for the use of the premises. Hire fees can include facilities in situ, such as existing sound and lighting, a certain level of staffing, the allocation of an in-house account manager or event co-ordinator, and existing furniture. It is important for the hirer to ascertain what is included within the hire fee and what other elements are charged for or will require hiring in.

Bringing elements in is not all that incurs costs. Care must be taken to ascertain the costs of elements which need to be removed or relocated to accommodate the event.

Some venues make a charge for the removal of furniture, or obstructions such as chandeliers that interfere with projection or sightlines.

Usually, the venue will require the full hire fee to be paid as the deposit, which secures the venue for the date of the event.

There should be no reason not to pay the full hire fee, unless the client is an individual, such as when organising a birthday party or wedding and it would be helpful to spread the cost.

Some venues require a percentage of the hire fee as the deposit, with subsequent payments due on specified dates until the hire fee is settled in full prior to the date of the event.

Most other costs associated with the venue, but which are not the hire fee – costs such as extra staff, technical requirements, furniture or flowers – will be payable prior to the event and some are payable after the event. This is because the hire fee and other pre-booked elements are fixed costs and are required to be paid before the event takes place, whereas other costs may be variable and will not be known until after the event.

Variable costs are due to the unconfirmed number of guests or delegates attending the event, and not knowing how much food or drink will be consumed. Thus, costs that get paid after the event are usually those that relate to food and beverages.

In most cases, the venue will require a date by which the event organiser must confirm the number of attendees. At this point, the variable charges become fixed and may be payable before the event takes place. This depends on the arrangement with the venue, their flexibility and their need for receiving the final number of attendees. In all cases, this should be stipulated within the venue contract.

5.2.1.7 Venue cancellation

If there is a need to cancel the booking of the venue, the contract will stipulate a cancellation fee structured according to how much notice of cancellation is given prior to the event date.

Each venue has its own cancellation policy, but the more time between the giving of the notice of cancellation and the event date, the less the client will need to pay. It works like this because the closer an event is, the less likely it is the venue will resell that date.

This is particularly relevant because events generally have a lengthy lead-in, so it is part of the planning process to know when would be best to cancel the venue should it prove necessary. If tickets are being sold for the event, for instance, a cut-off date should be identified where the number of tickets sold should break-even the costs, or generate a profit over costs. If this date arrives and the number of tickets to cover costs have not been sold, this is the date to cancel the event without incurring greater cancellation fees.

The event organiser (and the client) must acknowledge that events do get cancelled for all sorts of reasons.

Most event organisers and clients feel their event will not be cancelled. But, poor ticket sales or uptake of invitations could halt an event from going ahead. The weather is a common cause for having to cancel an event at short notice. The illness of a performer, or even their death, cannot be avoided. Insurance against accidents, loss and damage is required, of course, but it must be remembered to insure against cancellation when costs and charges have already been incurred.

Within the venue hire contract there could be written *get-in* and *get-out* times.

It is not safe to assume that the hire of a venue on Wednesday 24th March, say, allows access for the entirety of that date (the 24 hours of it). Many venues stipulate a 6 am get-in for deliveries and setting up (setting up includes decoration, stage dressing and rehearsals), but the get-in may be 8 am or even 12 midday, so this needs to be checked. Otherwise, deliveries and staff could be outside the venue without access to get in. This is not only inconvenient, but would incur staff wage costs and compromise the time needed to build the event before guests arrive.

The Natural History Museum in London has a *6 pm* get-in time, which is not uncommon with venues that are open to the public during the day. Visitors must be out before the event can get in.

Some venues have strict time restrictions because they are in sensitive areas, such as residential neighbourhoods that preclude late-night events. Other venues may have restricted access that can affect deliveries or guest arrivals by bus, taxi or limousine. Venues in London's Leicester Square, for example, have access gates that close at midday. Only emergency access or pre-arranged and approved VIP access is permitted after that hour.

Such restrictions and limitations are surmountable as long as the event organiser knows them in advance and has planned the logistics around them.

When booking the venue, care must be taken to consider rehearsal times. Many venues charge for rehearsal times, even when they fall within the paid-for hire period. This is because the venue needs to provide its sound and light facilities, and specialist technical crew and production manager from the beginning of the rehearsal onwards.

If there is a need to be in the venue for setting up before the event and breaking down after the event (also referred to as *load in* and *load out*), the venue should charge a reduced rate for such days or hours. This is reasonable because the venue cannot be used by anybody else during that period.

The usual fee for set-up (or *rigging*) and break-down days is 50% of the daily hire fee. But, this can vary and can also be negotiated.

If the event organiser has not paid a get-out fee to allow them time to de-rig or break-down the event, there can be steep financial penalties for the event overrunning or for failing to clear the venue within the contracted hire period. Check the small print of the hire contract because it is not unheard of for venues to increase their revenue by employing these tactics and charging per hour *after* the event has happened.

However, most venues use out-of-hours penalties as a deterrent so as to encourage clients to be prompt at getting out. It is dangerous practice for a venue to upset a client by actual additional charges after their event has happened.

It is worthwhile for the event organiser to check if there are any other bookings in the venue either side of their hire period. This is good practice because there may be a need to add a set-up day at a later point. And, it will determine whether the booking can be extended due to an overrun.

It may also be that furniture hire costs or stage costs can be shared between two clients at the one venue, rather than each paying full price for elements they could share. Suppliers should be happy with this because they will not have to collect from and deliver to the same venue more than once, which saves them costs.

Negotiation of the venue hire fee is based on factors such as repeat bookings. Maybe the event organiser has used the venue before, or wishes to book an annual event over the next year or three.

Negotiation is also possible depending on the duration of the booking. An exhibition over three or five days would expect to enjoy greater flexibility of the hire fee than a one-day booking might. Venues are similar to hotels in this respect; they rely on optimising their occupancy.

When determining the hire fee, the venue will also look at revenue from other income streams, such as bar and catering.

When the venue calculates its hire fee, the anticipated revenue from other streams will have an impact, such as sales of food and drink. If the event organiser can guarantee the venue that 500 people will be drinking, dining or staying overnight, the venue fee may even be waived. The venue will require a *guaranteed minimum spend* and the discounted or waived fee will kick in when the minimum spend is reached.

The level of hire fee can depend on the time of year or even the time of day. Venues do have their peak and off-peak periods. A nightclub, for example, would be more expensive for private hire on a Friday or Saturday evening than it would on a Monday evening.

Do not be surprised or argumentative if a public venue – even a public restaurant – demands an extortionate hire fee for private hire. It is loss of their regular business that is at stake plus the damage of goodwill with their regular clientele. A private-hire booking could impact the venue's regular public attendance for a week or two.

Another factor that can reduce the venue hire fee is celebrity and press attendance, where the event will provide the venue with an opportunity of gaining raised profile and publicity just by hosting the event. If the venue fears that another local venue may get the profile, the event organiser is in a strong bargaining position.

Charity events may receive a reduction in hire fees. Many venues have a standard percentage reduction in their fees for charity events, or they have a published charity rate.

Venues are extremely accommodating with their facilities and provisions when celebrities, press or high-profile charities are involved. But, some may be jaded and will doubt any claims of a huge press attendance and A-list celebrities. A central London venue may hear these claims every second week ... and such claims will usually be followed with a request for a zero hire fee.

The hire fee is for use of the premises only, during the hours on the day of the contract with the venue. This is why it is also known as a *facility fee* – it is the payment for use of the facility.

Other aspects the venue provides may or may not be included in the hire fee and this is another area which requires negotiation. The hire contract should list all equipment, facilities and staff that are included. In addition, there should be a price list for elements that are not included within the hire fee.

Well-equipped venues, such as conference centres and hotels, usually provide their in-house facilities within the cost of the hire fee. They feel this is the attraction for booking their venue. Besides, if items such as furniture and sound equipment are already on-site, there is no additional cost to the venue.

If this is the case, the venue hire fee could be considerably higher than a lesser-equipped venue so that the extras are paid for in a round-about way.

Even if a hire fee is inflated because of the facilities it includes, it can still be a saving from having to hire in essentials, like tables and chairs. Plus, there is no risk that the hired-in items do not get delivered, or the wrong item is delivered, or the wrong number is dropped and there are 50 chairs short, or the delivery gets caught in traffic and is late, or cannot park close to the venue ...

Hiring in from external sources increases risk, so it is always wise to use what is on-site.

Nevertheless, the event organiser must always check the venue's cost sheet for all other items that are charged – it may be cheaper to hire in than to use what is already there.

What a venue charges for and what is included in the hire fee can never be assumed. Just because a conference venue has a lectern and microphone, does not mean these items come within the hire fee. Wherever a venue realises a cost in providing facilities, said cost will be passed on to the hirer. Usually, this relates to staff, such as the sound and light technicians, a disc jockey, the amount of waiters required and how many hours the staff are required to work during the event.

5.3 Marketing

At some point early in the planning phase of an event, marketing needs to be carried out. This may be the responsibility of a marketing or PR agency – in which case the event organiser will need to liaise directly with them to ensure consistency in managing the event. Otherwise, the marketers may agree something that is unknown to the event organiser or is impossible to deliver.

In many cases, however, the event organiser is also responsible for marketing the event.

• • •

The rest of this section – on marketing and social media – is a contribution from Ashley Garlick.

There are many advanced tools that can be used when it comes to marketing, but in simplistic terms it can be boiled down to three M's: Market, Message, Medium.

Regardless of whether the event organiser is considering what might be called traditional marketing channels or newer digital channels, marketing always needs to consider the three M's.

5.3.1 Market

Whom is the event attempting to reach?

Usually this will be the customers or attendees. This needs to be thought through. Who are they? Where do they live? How old are they likely to be? What do they do for work or for fun? How educated are they?

Even details such as what car they drive or magazines they read will provide the market with an identity.

With a recurring event, this can be easily achieved by looking at who previous attendees were. It may also be that the client has given the event organiser a very specific brief about whom they want to attend, which again would make it easier to identify and reach that market. Even so, it is still necessary to find out as much about that market as possible.

Customers are never, ever just 'everybody'.

If the attendee base is very broad, it may help to split them into different groups. This will help to develop individual strategies for each group based on their common characteristics. This segmentation might be based on demographic, psychographic or behavioural attributes. For example, separating by age group, by values or by the benefits sought from the product or service.

5.3.2 Message

What is the event wanting to say to the audience?

There is some information that needs to be included – when it is happening, where it is happening and how much it will cost are usually the most important. But, there may be other vital messages depending on the individual event. This is especially significant if there are things the attendee needs to do or have before arriving at the event: for example, is there a dress code; will they need to book; or can they buy tickets on the door?

ASHLEY GARLICK'S VOICE BOX

I was approached by an event organiser producing a small charity event, who proudly wanted to show off their flyer, which they had printed several thousand times.

At first sight, things looked fine – it had a great design, and had all the key information.

When I checked the postcode, however, it turned out that it did not match the address of the event.

While they could mulch the remainder of the flyers, they had already distributed a large number to local residents.

They will never know how many potential attendees tried to go to their event, but ended up at the wrong place!

Always carefully proofread all your material, and check all your information is correct.

Once the content of the message is known, the tone of the message needs to be considered. Is the need to come across as professional or playful, informative or intriguing?

The tone should be relevant to the market. So, consider what would appeal to that market. The message may include visual elements – particularly as visual content generates more interest with consumers. If visual content is chosen, check that the pictures or graphics are relevant to the market, as well as being compatible with the event or company image.

The message should include a 'call to action'. This is something the customer will do after seeing the message. Do you want them to 'Like' your page or visit your website? Do you want them to buy a ticket or register for more information? The easier and more immediate your call to action, the more likely someone will do it.

5.3.3 Medium

This refers to the channel or channels you use to communicate your *message* to your *market*, and so should be directly informed by both these aspects.

When you know who your market is, you can consider the kind of places they will see you and your event. For example, if you know where your customers live and where they work, you can target sites on their commute such as bus routes or train advertisements. If you know they read a particular magazine or visit particular websites, you can target these.

You should also consider what the best medium is to convey your message. Do you need a video? In which case a YouTube channel might work.

Are pictures important? Then platforms such as Instagram or Pinterest may be best to use.

Two of the most common mediums are posters and flyers, as they can contain interesting visual material, as well as important information about the event. If using these, however, you must carefully consider where and when you will distribute them. When designing posters and flyers, they must grab the attention and interest of the viewer within a few seconds, and the viewer must be able to establish all the key facts in just a few seconds more.

5.3.4 Social media

The growth and influence of social media are undeniable. Event organisers are scrambling to get their events on a whole range of social media websites and apps. There are several reasons why . . .

Before the advent of social media, it was well-known that one of the most persuasive forms of advertisement was word-of-mouth. There was almost nothing as effective as a direct recommendation from one customer to another. Social media is seen to build on this, as new media platforms allow customers and potential customers to share their thoughts, feelings and experiences with a much greater number of people that can stretch far beyond the people they actually know. This transfer of direct communications has become known as 'super word-of-mouth'.

The sheer numbers of people using social media apps and websites make it a very attractive prospect for anyone trying to sell their wares to customers; event organisers are no different.

The technology behind these platforms also makes it easier than ever before to target your message to a very precise group of people, so understanding your market is more important than ever.

Some of the groups that use social media the most are also the same groups that do not respond to traditional forms of marketing, such as young people – this means that social media marketing is essential for companies wanting to target key demographics.

These platforms also make it easier to present traditional marketing as if you are coming as a recommendation from another customer; for example, someone liking a video you post on Facebook may appear to their friends as a direct endorsement of your event, even if they just liked the music used.

One misperception of social media marketing is that it is free marketing. While the direct cost of using social media is often far less than traditional advertising channels – especially when compared to platforms such as TV and radio – you should never assume you can successfully market your event for free. It may be possible to produce a campaign using only social media for no direct monetary cost, but event organisers often forget the real cost of time and effort. Effective social media marketing can be far more time-consuming than other channels, as it requires active engagement with your customers. Remember, your time is money – and doing social media 'right' takes far more time than many people realise.

The same rules apply to social media marketing as to traditional forms. You must consider your market, message and medium.

Know your customers well, and you will know which social media outlets they use most, and you can therefore target your efforts in the right places. Different people use different social media in very different ways. Unless you have a large marketing team, it can be very difficult to maintain a presence on every platform. Work out which ones are the most relevant and useful to your event, and put your efforts into these.

Unlike traditional forms of advertising, social media provides an opportunity for two-way, rather than one-way, communication. Many organisations with a presence on social media have a tendency to 'broadcast' information, whilst ignoring the opportunity to engage interactively with customers. Consider ways that you can capture and use content generated about your event by attendees or potential attendees.

Remember that events are all about experiences, and the experience of an event can begin well before the event itself. Capturing your customers' thoughts and feelings during the run-up can be a great way to build a buzz surrounding your event.

Equally, sharing positive experiences from the event itself helps establish a great relationship with your customers, as well as showing those who did not attend what they missed – making them more likely to buy a ticket next time round.

Like any campaign, an event organiser needs to approach social media with a clear strategy. Clear, simple and consistent messaging across multiple platforms makes it easier for people to cross-share to even more people.

While your ultimate goal may be to sell tickets for the event, you will find that an overtly sales-orientated approach does not go down well on social media. Consider what you are trying to achieve beyond making profit. Do you want to educate? How about encouraging people to share their experiences? Is it about generating conversation? Think about your broader goals and base your message around these.

With so much activity happening on social media, finding your event and making it stand out can be challenging. Plan your approach carefully and from the beginning. Hashtags have become a common way to make content more searchable on a number of different platforms. Make sure you have considered unique key words you can use, and ensure that you show these clearly and consistently in your material. That said, some of the most influential activity often comes from users, so be responsive during your campaign to emerging trends that you can incorporate into your own activity.

5.3.4.1 Search engine optimisation (SEO)

A growing area of interest to digital and social media marketing experts is called search engine optimisation (SEO).

SEO refers to the process of designing digital content in such a way as to maximise the chances of it being returned in the top results of a search engine (such as Google or Bing).

It is an approach that has come about as search engines have emerged as one of the most dominant ways by which people navigate the Internet, and as the algorithms used by different engines have become more sophisticated.

Given the amount of data that companies such as Google collect about browsing and searching habits, they have become skilled at the precision targeting of relevant information to users; therefore, if your material is well-designed and constructed with them in mind, search engines can become powerful tools to direct your event to exactly the right people who may be interested.

Broadly speaking, most search engines determine the strength of a particular site or source in terms of two primary factors: relevance and popularity.

You can improve the relevance of your material by using clear terms in titles, headings and web-pages. Well-designed hashtags encourage more widespread and consistent use of unique phrases, which help link your online content with your consumers. Popularity is largely driven by traffic. The more people are interested in your content, the more likely other people will be interested as well.

'Clicks', 'likes' and 'shares' have become common ways to explicitly demonstrate popularity and as such have become some of the most common 'calls to action'. Most social media platforms will have these, or an equivalent, that you can make use of in your campaign.

Some services offer the opportunity to *buy* popularity; while these can sometimes be an effective way to build early momentum, they should always be used with caution, as often such momentum does not represent real interest. If the content is not engaging for people, it will not generate the desired return of increased attendance – no matter how much you spend.

5.4 Funding

Funding for an event comes from one of four sources:

- the client purse
- sponsors
- exhibitors
- paying guests.

Additionally, funding can come from government, grants, philanthropy, and lottery-funded. There could also be self-funded events (such as promoting a hotel to event clients) and, potentially, crowd-funded events. The term 'paying guests' may be ticket or admission charges and/or it could be cash sales at an event, such as bars, food outlets, merchandise or guests purchasing items at an exhibition.

Every event – even one that is not about making money, such as a press briefing – will incur costs that need to be covered from one of the aforementioned sources.

5.4.1 The client purse

Either the client will set the budget before the event organiser prepares the proposal (which proposes the anticipated costs), or the budget will be generated by the building of the proposal itself. The former is a budget given by the client, whereas the latter is a budget presented by the event organiser.

A client may know how much they wish to spend on an event, or they may want the event organiser to tell them how much an event will cost.

Many times, a client will not know how much the elements of an event will cost, so they will be relying on the event organiser to guide them.

The difficulty for the event organiser is not learning how much the client wishes to spend until after the proposal has been submitted. The fear factor when writing a proposal, is feeling that if the proposed budget is too high, the event organiser will lose the job because it is too expensive.

So, the event organiser may be bent into pitching a lower budget to win the job. This may delight the client, but it could result in the event organiser having a struggle to bring the event within budget, or having to compromise standards if the low budget proves unrealistic.

5.4.2 Sponsors

If funding for the event is coming from sponsorships, it must be ascertained who is responsible for engaging the sponsors.

Ideally, the client will have relationships with potential sponsors, and the manpower to engage them and manage the relationship. This is usually the case because the client's event will likely be in a specific field of industry, which will attract the appropriate sponsors and capitalise on existing relationships and networks.

In all cases, the client should involve the event organiser with the sponsors to discuss their needs and requirements at the event, such as branding; positioning of bar stock; prizes, sampling or demonstrations; and colour, theme and hospitality. It is the control thing again: the event organiser must control everything. It would not be good event management if the client were allowed to promise things to sponsors that cannot be delivered, that are not within budget or that the event organiser knew nothing about until the day of the event.

It helps if the event organiser is involved with the design of sponsorship packages as he is the one who knows what is achievable, how to achieve it and where to allocate it within the event budget.

Sponsor hospitality packages may include pre-event cocktails, a canapé reception or a post-event party for the sponsor company's guests, clients or its own executives.

There is an example sponsor package in Appendix II.

Sponsors sometimes feel they are king-makers and that they own the event. They may feel that the event would not happen without their sponsorship. So, the event organiser becomes charged with satisfying the client, the sponsor(s) and all the guests! It is a difficult ask, and it is worthwhile to remember that the sponsor is the 'real' client when dealing with sponsorship issues.

5.4.2.1 Types of sponsor

There are four types of sponsor.

The first is the main sponsor (*headline* sponsor or *title* sponsor). The 'headline' or 'title' denotes that the sponsor's name gets incorporated into the title of the event, e.g. The *EE* Bafta Awards or The *Mastercard* Brit Awards.

The headline sponsor's package will be more expensive than any other sponsors and will provide more benefits and profile than any other sponsor packages.

The second type of sponsor is the *satellite* sponsors. These are a range of sponsors that pay a lesser fee than the headline sponsor and they receive a lesser package. At an event there may be more than one of this type of sponsor and up to as many as 20, say, individual sponsors. Hence the term 'satellite' sponsors. These sponsors can be identified usually at the bottom of flyers, posters, invitations and tickets as a row of corporate logos and brands.

The third type of sponsor is the *media* sponsor (*media partner*). These will be magazine or newspaper titles, or television channels that do not pay for their sponsorship package but have a contra deal, where they provide coverage of the event and in return receive a package such as tickets to the event or exclusivity backstage.

The fourth type of sponsor is the *donor* – one who donates products or services to the event. These sponsors will not pay cash to cover costs of the event, but rather supply their brands or services in return for a profile at the event, being associated with the event or receiving a benefit such as attending the event.

AUTHOR'S VOICE BOX

I once received a brief to provide canapés for Elton John's White Tie and Tiara Ball at his opulent Windsor mansion.

It was in aid of the Elton John Aids Foundation, which is a notable charity for a good cause, so I was eager to help.

But, the brief called for separate themed menus for each of Elton's themed gardens and the logistics were costly – in particular the food and staffing costs.

The event brief stipulated that all suppliers were expected to supply their services for free, so that the charity incurred less cost. So, I had to decide not to take the unpaid job. It disappointed me because the profile and potential business connections at such a prestigious event may have been worth the expense. But, I am an event organiser, not a sponsor.

5.4.3 Exhibitors

Exhibitions are organised for targeted attendees who are interested in whatever is being exhibited whether it is toys, new products in a certain market, Christmas gifts or computer games.

The exhibitors will pay for their space and presence to reach that target market.

The charge made to exhibitors to be there will be the main income stream for the exhibition organiser and will cover the costs (such as the exhibition venue) and generate profit.

There can be many exhibitors at one exhibition – each paying for their space. All exhibitors will pay for the standard basic package. This could be a table with a cloth, or a *shell scheme*. A shell scheme usually consists of the space, walls, basic furniture and flooring.

The price an exhibitor pays will depend upon the size of the space they book and the location of the space. For example, a 12 m x 12 m space near the main entrance will cost more than a 3 m x 3 m space at the back of the hall.

The exhibition organiser will increase their revenue by add-ons to the basic shell scheme. These add-ons may be electricity, phone sockets, extra furniture, carpeting, a ceiling, lighting or data-capture facilities.

5.4.4 Paying guests

5.4.4.1 Tickets

If the event is being funded by guests who pay for admission, this can be either through the purchase of tickets in advance, or 'on the door' on the day of the event. This structure of funding is most common with concerts, craft markets, antiques fairs and exhibitions that charge for entry.

Remember, this is the business of minimising risk, so it is always better to sell tickets in advance and be assured of how many people are committed to attending the event. Selling tickets on the door is high-risk because the event organiser will not know how many people will turn up for the event, and will also not know how much revenue the ticket sales will generate.

Clearly, if too few arrive to buy tickets on the day, the event risks bankruptcy because the costs could outweigh the door receipts. There is another risk with selling tickets on the door: it would be disastrous to have 1,000 guests queuing to buy tickets on the door on the day of the event when the venue capacity is only 800. It would be very damaging to the reputation of the event (and the event organiser) if guests turn up but are not admitted and have to leave disappointed and angry.

It is vital to reduce the ambiguity of how many guests will attend an event.

If the ticket price is considered low, or the tickets are free, there is a further increased risk of ticket-holders not attending the event on the day. This is the perceived value of the ticket. It is a situation which occurs when the weather turns nasty, there is a transport strike or a competing event is happening on the same day.

To prevent this happening, a mechanism should be introduced that provides the event organiser with a gauge of how many guests are likely to attend the event. Such mechanisms can include invitations with a lucky number on each and automatic entry into a draw for a chance to win a prize, or having to respond to the invitation to get entered into the prize draw. It will not be exact, but will go some way towards anticipating the number of guests to expect and lessening the risk.

5.4.4.2 Other revenue streams

Other ways of raising funds during an event include raffles, prizes, auctions, cash bars, cash food and paid-for entertainment such as games and fairground rides.

5.5 Theme

Often, there is a theme to an event and this is important to ascertain at the briefing meeting – unless the client has briefed the event organiser to suggest themes.

Even seasonal events such as Christmas parties can have different themes: winter wonderland, Snow White, traditional Christmas, woodland Christmas, Alpine Christmas or a theme around a Christmas movie.

Many event organisers prefer themed events because it allows them to input their creativity. It also provides additional revenue from the hired-in extras that are needed to enhance a theme.

Building any theme impacts the budget because it will require costume hire, set building, prop hire and decoration. It may also demand specialist decorators and technical logistics.

But, developing a theme runs further than the budget. It may determine the style of venue, staff uniform, entertainment, time of year and even the menu choice.

The main point of themes for events is that they enhance the guest experience – at what are called *experiential* events.

Although people understand what is meant when a party is themed, themes are employed for events that are staged for things other than fun – to commemorate a historical event, for example.

Themes are also used to make an event memorable, or to fit with a brand or product.

A film premiere will almost always be themed to fit the style or title of the film, and a music album launch will be themed to suit the title of the album or the profile of the band.

For a straightforward sales conference, a theme can be used to identify the product, or sales targets, or the location of the conference . . . or even the year it is taking place so that delegates remember the conference not only by the year it took place, but also for its theme.

5.5.1 Themed proposals

Some event organisers choose to submit themed proposals in menu fashion. This means they will list three proposed themes that meet a lower cost, mid-range cost and high-end cost.

The client can select the theme that appeals to them and their budget. For example, a circus-themed event, with acrobats, fire-eaters, entertainers and a ring-master, would cost more than a Victorian seaside theme with a puppet theatre, candy floss and a winkle stall.

Some themes are cheaper to produce than others. Some are standard off-the-shelf themes, such as an 80s theme. Whereas, other themes require much more input and individual creativity, such as a Harry Potter theme or a Formula 1 theme.

5.6 The client file

The need to produce and keep a client file for each event was born from the need to create a paper trail. Nevertheless, it is still necessary for the event organiser to create a virtual pathway during the planning process, which can be followed on a touch-screen tablet.

The only real difference here is the ease of carrying a tablet on-site instead of carrying a ring binder with papers, contact lists, memos, menus, order forms, contact reports, contracts and every other document that gets put into the client file.

Because the nature of event management necessitates drawing many components together, and because the lead-in can be three months or longer, it is necessary to file all communications. Otherwise, things get forgotten or overlooked.

Every decision that is made by the client must be recorded. So must the discussions and negotiations with suppliers, contractors and the venue. Every detail must be recorded and retained.

Some event organisers write client contact reports to record what was discussed and agreed during client meetings, who was present and when the meeting took place. Contact reports are helpful if there is a dispute with a client at a later date and you need to refer to what was said at the time.

The client file should be constructed in order of the process. The enquiry form will be at the front. Next, will be notes from the briefing meeting. Then come the proposal, the client confirmation, the venue contract, the catering order etc.

At the end of the client file will be notes from the client debriefing meeting, the office debriefing meeting and lastly the final report. These are discussed in Part 4.

The client file is not only about good administration management. As the plans for the event come together, the client file will grow and become the event organiser's bible. This is the file that accompanies the event organiser to the event itself.

Within, the client file should contain the orders for each supplier, so that when the chairs, say, are delivered on-site the organiser can refer to how many were ordered, when they were ordered and who took the order. If anything goes wrong on the day, the organiser needs such information to hand. Also, the client file should contain a contact list, so that the organiser can contact all suppliers from the event site.

There is an additional advantage to keeping client files, which is that they are useful for other events. Often, the information contained in one client file will be useful for another. This helps immensely with research during the proposal and budgeting stages of a future enquiry.

Sometimes, a client may wish to repeat an event – even if it does not appear evident at the time of the initial event. So, it is worthwhile to generate a comprehensive client file . . . and retain it.

Chapter **6**

Catering and beverages

6.1 Catering

Key to every event is the provision of food and drink – not only because everybody knows good food from bad food, but because it is a legal requirement to serve food when serving alcohol.

At the proposal stage it is a simple matter to obtain menus and calculate the menu cost per person (*per head* or *per capita*) and from this the overall cost of catering for the total amount of guests attending. Menus and food costs can be obtained from venues or caterers. However, it may not even be necessary to contact a caterer to obtain costs at the proposal-building stage, but simply cast a glance at a previous client file and ascertain costs from similar menu styles.

Sometimes an event organiser will need to obtain specific menus and costs from a caterer so as to build the budget proposal – particularly if the brief is for a themed event.

As with every element of an event, if there is a problem it reflects negatively on the event organiser, the client and the venue. Because catering is key to the success of an event – and because everybody judges food when they eat it – most event organisers will only work with caterers they can rely on from previous experience. Reliance is not only about food quality, for good catering requires excellent hygiene, good timing, logistics, service, provision of equipment and clearing up afterwards.

6.1.1 In-house catering

If the venue has catering in-house, they will require the event organiser to use it. It makes sense to do so, because the in-house catering team will understand the idiosyncrasies of the venue, for one thing. Also, it can be simpler and cheaper to employ the in-house catering team; they're already there.

Another thing to consider is that it is the in-house catering team's kitchen and equipment, and they may not wish to entrust them to an outside caterer. In addition, chefs are notoriously defensive, possessive and competitive. An organiser who insists on *not* using the in-house team risks conflict with the kitchen brigade and a situation of non-cooperation between the in-house caterers and the one sourced externally.

The venue may genuinely wish for their in-house catering team to be used so as to ensure catering standards are upheld at their venue. From the guest point of view, a poor meal reflects poorly on the venue. So, a good venue will not wish for their reputation to suffer by forgoing control of what is served from their kitchen.

Although it is logistically easier, less risky and usually cost-beneficial to use the venue's in-house catering, there are reasons *not* to use the in-house caterer. It could be that the in-house menus are costlier than an external food provider. Or, perhaps the chosen venue has a poor reputation for its catering provision. It could be that the event organiser – or the client – has a relationship with an external event caterer because they prefer their food provision, they get a discount or they receive commission. Sometimes, an event requires specialist catering, such as kosher, which needs to be sourced externally. But, wherever possible, it is best to use in-house catering.

Some venues prohibit external caterers at their premises. This is because the venue loses revenue from food sales. To counteract the revenue loss, such venues (but not all) will charge for external catering to be brought in. This is usually charged per head (for each guest) and can make the catering costs unfeasible if paying for an external caterer *and* having to pay the venue a fee for using an external caterer.

Some venues intentionally charge an unfeasibly high fee to deter an event organiser from bringing in an external caterer. This will encourage use of their in-house catering.

6.1.2 Outside catering

If there is no in-house catering, it does not mean the event organiser can bring in just any caterer. A good venue will still want to protect its reputation.

The venue will issue a list of approved caterers from which the event organiser may select.

It may be that the event organiser is familiar with one or more caterers on the approved list. If not, it will be a matter of trusting the venue's selection of caterers and ensuring that a menu tasting takes place.

If the venue does not have in-house catering, or if the event organiser is bringing in external caterers, or if the event is on a green-field site where there are no facilities anyhow, it is simple to find event caterers. They are abundant and all event directories provide such information.

Selecting which event caterer to use is down to reputation, experience and testimonials. Other than these, there is menu tasting.

6.1.3 Menu tasting

Venues and event caterers will be happy to tailor menus to suit the event brief. Most caterers and venues will also arrange a menu tasting. This is particularly worthwhile to ascertain the quality of catering. A menu tasting also ascertains how easy the food is to serve and be eaten (the latter being particularly relevant with canapé menus – canapés must be neither too large nor too messy to eat); how the food presents itself on the plate or platter; the colour of food items, which may not be to the liking of the client; and the taste of dishes. All these elements can be deduced at a menu tasting during the planning stages of the event.

AUTHOR'S VOICE BOX

Be wary when taking clients to a menu tasting. I once attended a tasting in a luxury hotel on Park Lane with a gaggle of girls who walked into the tasting suite and announced how 'starving' they all were. They scoffed every plate and mopped up the crumbs.

It is unprofessional to be hungry at a menu tasting. The venue or caterer is extending a courtesy and its purpose is to sample, taste and judge the menu – not to stuff yourself on free food.

The event organiser may invite the client to the menu tasting as a social interaction and to include the client's views on this key element of their event.

6.1.4 Types of catering

There are just three types of catering styles.

6.1.4.1 Buffet

A buffet is a table of dishes.

A *finger buffet* is where the food is easy to pick up and eat, such as cocktail sausages and vol-au-vents.

A *fork buffet* is more substantial and requires a fork. Such buffet dishes may include individual pots of curry and rice, for example. Often, a fork buffet will necessitate guests to sit and eat once they have visited the buffet.

Buffets do allow guests to interact and are suitable for relaxing the formality of an event. On the downside, buffets can create queues for food, which guests dislike. It is a good idea to set up more than one buffet table for larger events. The dessert dishes can be on a different table, too. And, disperse guests by providing cutlery and condiments on separate tables from the buffet so that the flow is quicker.

Cold platters will be placed on silver trays (or *flats*). Hot foods will be served from lidded *chafing dishes* that are partially filled with water which is heated electrically or by gel-candle burners underneath. The heated water keeps the food hot but does not burn the food by direct heat. Even so, the food should be stirred occasionally to distribute the heat and prevent the top food from drying out. It is also important to keep an eye on the water level so that it does not dry out.

Buffets may be self-service for the guests to help themselves, or they can be served by staff from behind the buffet table. If portion control and speed of service are important, it is advisable to have waiters serving the guests. It is also a courteous gesture should a guest have any questions about the food items.

Although it is common to see a buffet table set against a wall, the table should *always* allow room for staff members to get behind and remove or replenish dishes. There is nothing ruder than a waiter having to disrupt queuing guests by cutting through with platters of food.

If space allows, the buffet table should be well away from the walls so that guests may approach from both sides. This is not only more convenient for guests, it speeds up service and reduces queue lengths, and is also more sociable.

Care must be taken to replenish the dishes on the buffet to ensure the food is kept fresh and does not grow overcooked or tired.

Half-empty trays are unappealing and suggest the food has been there a while. Once a flat or a chafing dish is half empty, it should be returned to the kitchen for replenishing.

The last guest at the buffet table should receive the same first-class experience as the first guest.

6.1.4.2 Banquet or sit-down dinner

This style of catering is for formal events and tends to be used for larger occasions because of the space required and the time it takes for waiters to serve the meal.

Banquets are suitable for events with a stage or presentation because it keeps the formalities tight and will assist with strict timings, whilst also providing every guest with a seat from where to see the stage. This is a *gala banquet*.

The banqueting manager can brief the waiters on the speed of service and when they must leave the room (or *clear the floor*) because the show or presentation is ready to start.

The seating arrangements for a banquet will require a table plan so that guests know where to sit for their meal.

Seating can be arranged on round tables (*banqueting rounds*) that by standard are either 5 ft in diameter for 10 guests per table, or 6 ft in diameter for 12 guests per table.

Otherwise, long tables (*trestles*) can be joined to seat any number of guests.

Some banquets require a top table for VIP guests (such as the bride and groom at a wedding) and additional offshoot tables (*sprigs*).

It should be noted that where an event organiser does *not* want to highlight a special or VIP table, the layout and seating plan will not show a Table No.1. The plan will start with Table 2. This is usual where VIPs host tables or the organiser wishes *all* guests to be 'VIPs'.

Furthermore, it is common not to have a Table No.13 due to superstition.

So, the event organiser must communicate the *actual amount* of tables if there is not a Table 1 and not a Table 13. This is important for the caterer, chef, waiting staff and technical crew if they are spot-lighting guests at an award ceremony, for example.

At a banquet the waiters serve from trays onto the seated diner's plate using a spoon and fork – this is *silver service*.

Or, platters of food are placed at the centre of each table and guests help themselves – this is *tray service*.

Or, food is ready-plated for each guest and waiters simply place the plate in front of the seated guest – this is *plate service*.

Or, the meat is already on each plate, but platters of vegetables are placed at the centre of each table – this is *family service*.

It is customary to schedule a 15-minute *comfort break* to allow guests to visit the cloakroom. This usually happens with the service of coffee. On formal occasions, gentlemen should not remove their jackets (or light their cigars) until the comfort break is announced.

It is important to inform guests of the comfort break and also to recall them to their seats afterwards. A toastmaster (or *Master of Ceremonies*, or *MC*) will make the announcements. Otherwise a voice on the microphone will make such announcements – this voice is referred to as the 'Voice of God' or 'VOG'.

If a toastmaster is hosting the banquet, he would be served his meal at the same time as the guests and in the same room, but at a separate table.

Sometimes, coffee will be served at the commencement of the stage presentation or show. This should only be when timing is tight, because the service and noise of teacups and teaspoons are distracting.

Ideally, waiters should serve coffee before the comfort break and clear the tables during the comfort break. At the end of the comfort break, the waiters can leave the room.

A good banqueting manager will brief his staff to follow his lead, and the waiters would neither serve, nor clear, until directed.

Remember, half the guests at a banquet will be seated with their back to the stage. So, if there is a lengthy show and this is going to be a problem, there may be an opportunity to arrange *cabaret-style* seating, where all chairs around each table face the stage (which means half the guests have their backs to the *table* and not the stage). Or, if the venue affords the space, only half of each table is set and used.

In other cases, and again if the size of the venue allows, it is advisable to have *theatre-style* rows of chairs for the stage show, and to hold the banquet in an adjoining space.

It should be noted that rows of theatre-style chairs will require fixing to each other or the floor. This is a legal safety requirement in case of the emergency evacuation of guests.

6.1.4.3 Canapés

Canapés are bite-sized pieces of food that can be savoury or sweet. They should be visually appealing and easy to eat.

Canapés are most often served from trays by waiters circulating among the guests. This is labour-intensive and requires good management of the staff to ensure they reach every area of the room. Waiters will need to carry cocktail napkins, as well.

Or, the canapés can be laid onto a table, like a buffet, and guests can help themselves.

The canapé style of service encourages guests to circulate, such as at parties, cocktail receptions, film premieres and high-quality social events.

Canapés are suitable for offering hospitality without having to provide a substantial meal. It is therefore a suitable style of menu in venues with restricted space or when the catering budget does not allow for substantial food to be served. However, canapé menus can be expensive, too.

In very crowded environments the service of canapés can be restrictive and a small proportion of the guests may not see a canapé during the event. Whereas, the knowledgeable or lucky guest will stand close to the kitchen and be the first to be met by the waiters. It is a common problem for some guests to leave an event without having been served.

It is advisable not to serve canapés too early. Doing so may mean that the first guests to arrive eat heartily, but the later arrivals taste nothing. The best time to begin canapé service is when the arrival of guests has slowed. It is also a good idea to stagger the service so that waiters leave the floor for a while before commencing the second service of canapés.

6.1.5 Catering logistics

Once the choice of event caterer has been agreed, the caterer may wish to view the venue to ascertain access routes, equipment required and the service logistics, and may also wish to view the venue before the menu is agreed.

The event organiser must be present at such visits. If not, the caterer will liaise with the venue – and the event organiser has already lost control.

The caterer will need to know the number of guests expected to attend the event. In the early stages of planning, this will be an estimated figure.

At an agreed date closer to the event (usually seven days prior, but not always), the caterer will require confirmed catering numbers.

If the confirmed number of guests is not known, the caterer will at least need to know the guaranteed minimum number of guests who require food. This will be the contractual number that the caterer will charge, but the final total number may be higher. So, if the guaranteed minimum number is 100, the caterer can invoice catering for 100 guests and this will be paid before the event. If the actual number on the day of the event is 115 guests, the catering invoice will be for 115 guests. Whereas, if the actual number of guests turns out to be 94, the caterer has already been paid for 100 guests (or will invoice for 100 guests) because that was the guaranteed minimum number.

Bear in mind that the catering numbers may not correspond to the number of guests, because catering could be required for press, crew, staff, and perhaps also during rehearsals. Maybe the crew's breakfast and lunch will require serving during the day. An event caterer would usually charge a reduced rate for staff and crew food.

Caterers may charge for the amount of plates served, not people. This means that where there may be 100 guests, 25 of them could have visited the buffet twice, thus the caterer will charge not for 100 guests, but for 125 plates served.

If the caterer is going to charge for how many people actually attend the event, the event organiser must verify this information themselves. It cannot be left up to the caterer to count the guests, because it is in the caterer's interest to inflate the number.

Likewise, the venue has an interest to inflate the number of guests attending, because the bar spend will reflect how many people are in the venue. So, even though the venue's own door staff will count the guests (it is the venue's legal duty to monitor attendance so as not to exceed their legal capacity), the event organiser cannot rely on their count either.

Additionally, a caterer will always over-cater because there must not be a risk of the food running out during the event. If the event organiser confirms numbers at 100 and the caterer over-caters by 20%, the caterer may wish to claw back the cost of providing those extra meals that otherwise do not get paid for because they were not ordered.

In all cases, the event organiser must have a member of their event team independently verify the number of guests attending an event.

6.2 Beverages

Most venues have existing bars in situ (except unusual venues and green-field sites). Even so, it is wise to always assess the number of guests and the flow of activities.

Sometimes, it is necessary to erect satellite bars to ease congestion. This is particularly important in venues that may not normally expect all the guests to arrive at one time.

When in the process of a venue reconnaissance (*recce*), the event organiser must walk through the venue and envisage the flow of guests and the activities taking place. For example, if a conference is going to break for lunch are the bars sufficient to cope with the sudden influx of delegates? This is important for the guests' experience of the service, but there is an additional need to ensure everybody is served before the conference resumes.

There will be additional pressure on bars if the drinks are free.

If temporary bars are being set up, they should be positioned deep inside the venue to draw guests to the back of the space, wherever possible.

AUTHOR'S VOICE BOX

I attended a prestigious celebrity party that was held in an empty, dilapidated house. The disc jockey was spinning discs in the living room and the bar was set up in the kitchen.

However, the kitchen was too small to accommodate the crowds at the bar. But, this is where the crowd wanted to be because of the bar.

This resulted in the kitchen being overcrowded and the disc jockey being in the lounge by himself.

It was too late to relocate the bar. Instead, I interfered and suggested to the DJ that he reduce the volume and beats per minute so that guests were encouraged to escape the overcrowded environment of the kitchen and seek relaxation in the lounge with lounge music.

I was surprised that the DJ took my advice. And, within a few moments guests filtered from the kitchen into the living room.

This small intervention alleviated the crush at the bar and gave the DJ his audience.

The event organiser must take care not to be tempted to place bars where people congregate, such as beside a dance-floor, close to toilet areas or near the disc jockey. These may at first seem obvious places to site a bar when the venue is in preparation and is empty, but will cause congestion and blockages when the venue is full.

The event organiser must also ensure that the venue or caterer is providing enough bar staff for the number of guests and the flow. Busy times will be arrival, conference breaks, conference end, pre-dinner and after dinner.

Nobody enjoys waiting to be served.

At banquets and formal dinners, guests are served drinks at their table. This is largely for convenience. But, it does prevent guests constantly visiting the bar like ants that have discovered a food source. Where possible, guests should be seated – especially if space is limited. Weddings particularly fall foul of this rule and the banqueting suite can be half empty because guests are creating a second event at the bar.

Even if the bar is in the same room as the banquet, waiters should serve drinks to guests at tables. Otherwise, the bar becomes a distraction.

If drinks are provided free of charge or by a drinks sponsor, it is acceptable to place a package of drinks on each table for the guests to help themselves. The sponsor will appreciate the exposure of the drink brand(s). But, each table must receive the same drinks package. The package of drinks is usually presented in ice buckets because it would usually require chilled drink products.

It is important not to leave too large a package on tables: greed sets in, which impacts guest behaviour when mixed with alcohol. It also results in much product wastage, such as half-consumed bottles of wine. It is far better to have waiters continually topping up the table drinks packages when required.

At events where a stage activity is happening – presentations, conferences, launches, fashion shows, entertainment – it is a mistake to open the bar before the end of the show.

If the bar opens before the show, guests will begin drinking and getting loud. They will also very quickly create a side-event at the bar which will detract from the show or purpose of the event.

Even opening a bar during a show is a risk. Guests who are intent on watching the show or listening to the presenter will be distracted by the noise of bar service and people chatting or ordering drinks.

6.2.1 Welcome drinks

It is usual to welcome guests to the event with wine, a cocktail or glass of champagne. For this, it is common practice to station waiters with trays of drinks close to the door.

This is a logistical error that occurs with such regularity that it has become an epidemic of wrongness.

The entrance has a purpose and it is not socialising. It is for arrivals, registration, security, checking guest lists, checking passes . . . the very last thing to add to the bedlam of activity is waiters with welcome drinks.

Besides all this activity, if guests are stopped at the entrance and given a drink, this is where they will linger. They will then meet friends as more guests enter the venue. People will stand and make conversation which only heaps chaos upon bedlam. Blockages occur and the event is already in mayhem – right from the very beginning.

The savvy event organiser will position the waiters with welcome drinks deep inside the venue. This will draw guests into the venue and away from the entrance and cloakroom, which are the busiest areas at the beginning of the event. Anyway, it is far more welcoming for a guest to be invited *into* the venue for a drink rather than given one at the front door. It is inconvenient to be burdened with a drink whilst removing a coat or looking for the cloakroom.

Once guests begin to fill the venue, the drinks waiters can move closer and closer to the front entrance. This means that the venue fills quickly and is not looking empty, and it frees the front entrance.

Waiters should never serve welcome drinks from trays. It is a tradition that does not work.

On so many occasions, waiters are forced to hold full trays of champagne flutes and their arms give way without them even realising it is happening. It is an endurance feat that is purely unnecessary and results in embarrassment for the poor waiter, and a logistical difficulty to clear the spilt champagne and broken glass.

The event organiser must lessen the risk by having welcome drinks ready-poured on a table well inside the venue (or two tables – one either side of the entrance if there is space, but not too close to the front doors). Waiters with a glass or two of drinks on trays will serve some of the guests as a courtesy, but guests may collect their welcome drink from the table. This will dramatically speed the entrance flow of guests and prevent the waiters from standing with overloaded trays and aching arms.

When serving complimentary wine, it is common practice for waiters to circulate with trays of wine poured into glasses. Again, this is a logistical error.

It is far better to allow guests to select their choice of wine at the welcome table and thereafter be served by waiters circulating with a *bottle* of red wine and a *bottle* of white wine. This way, guests consistently receive a top-up without having to return to the drinks table. Also, there is zero demand for fresh glasses that otherwise would need collecting and washing. Additionally, guests retain their glass for the top-up and so the venue does not become littered with used glasses, which would require additional staff to clear.

On top of all these benefits for a simple adjustment of wine service, it is additionally a good way of displaying the wine label to guests. If the drink has been donated by a sponsor, the sponsor will be delighted at the exposure of the label.

6.2.2 Sponsored drinks

As early as the briefing stage it needs to be considered who is supplying the drinks and whether the guests will be paying for them.

The advertising of alcohol is legally restricted to age-appropriate markets and age-targeted audiences. This means that the drinks companies and drink brands are keen to promote their products at events where the audience profile and demographics are known. The drinks company will identify whether their brand(s) suit the target audience attending the event.

A drinks company will also be keen to direct-sample drink brands – especially new brands – to a direct market where the consumer gets to taste the product. This is important for awareness. But even traditional, known drink brands are promoted in this way to remind consumers of the product or to get them to taste what they would not usually ask for when out for a drink.

Often, a drinks company will also supply branded bars, staff uniforms and branded *point-of-sale* (POS) material, such as ice buckets, drip mats and glassware, to support the identity of their brands.

Drinks sponsorship is widespread in the events industry, particularly where the drinks brand will receive promotion, such as at televised or high-interest press events. Usually, such events are charity or celebrity-attended occasions, when there is a possibility that a paparazzi photograph of Elton John holding a Belvedere vodka glass will reach the newspapers and celebrity websites.

It is not always the celebrity market that is being targeted by drinks companies, however. The mass market is the prize. So, local events enjoy drinks sponsorship too. At all types of events there are branded bars, or Coca-Cola ice buckets, say.

Although drinks companies are valued friends of event organisers because of the product they donate, it is rare for a drinks company to give cash. Even if the drinks company is sizeable and cash-rich, they do not like to give money and they would rather donate product. This way, they are promoting their product without hard cost.

Whenever there is a drinks sponsor, the event organiser must be careful to notify the venue because many venues are contractually tied to their own suppliers and cannot sell, stock or even display a drink supplier's competitor brand. This applies to soft drinks as well as alcohol.

Also, any donated or give-away drink products will affect the venue's bar income during the event. This, in turn, will impact the venue hire fee. So, this must be taken into account early in the planning stages.

A venue will always quote their hire fee based on expected revenue from food and drink. So, if the drinks are going to be supplied by a sponsor and there is also an outside caterer, the venue fee will be high to account for loss of income from these other streams.

With drinks sponsorship the venue will usually accept a 'one-for-one' arrangement. This is where each bottle of whisky, for example, which is provided by the drinks sponsor for the event, is matched by a bottle of whisky being given to the venue for their cellar stock. In effect, the venue receives a bottle of whisky free and can make money on it by selling it at another time. So, if the requirement is 12 bottles of gin and 12 bottles of whisky donated for guests at the event, and the venue has agreed a one-for-one deal, the event organiser must arrange for 24 bottles of gin and 24 bottles of whisky from the drinks provider. This allows the venue to later recoup the sale of gin and whisky at a later date to make up for the loss of sales at the event because the drinks were free and there was no bar income.

All this has to be predetermined by the event organiser. If there is a contractual obligation not to stock another drink supplier's product, the venue may be permitted to give the product away at a private event. However, the venue will not be allowed to retail that stock at a later date.

If it should seem too generous to give the venue one bottle for its cellar stock for each bottle donated for use at the event, it should be remembered that the venue's half of the deal is not without cost. The venue will need to receive delivery of the donated stock, store it, secure it and serve it. In addition, the venue will need to clear the bars of existing stock, restock with the donated product and replace its own stock after the event.

Caution must be taken when donated alcohol product is provided for an event. A venue will view donated stock as prized manna from heaven: it can make all the profit without any cost.

So, the event organiser must find a way of monitoring the stock during the event. Otherwise, a bottle or two will be skimmed from the donated product and assimilated into the venue's own stock. If the product is bottled beer, a case or two may be whisked away.

Alcoholic product is always a highly prized commodity and bottles or cases of alcohol can disappear into a venue manager's office or hiding places. A seasoned event organiser will ask to view the product on-site and count it, then monitor how quickly it is being consumed. It is not unknown for venue managers to declare there is no product left when there is a consignment tucked away out of sight, which the sponsor has donated for the purpose of brand profile to the guests and which was meant for guests to enjoy.

If drink product runs out during an event, it is a catastrophe. Event organisers know this and can be held to ransom by a venue. This will mean increasing the bar budget (which increases the venue's revenue) or being forced to purchase the venue's own stock.

6.2.3 Drinks supplied by the venue

If the venue is supplying the drinks, it can be just as unscrupulous – dealing with alcohol always is.

Paying the bar account after the event is often a problem – *most* often, it is a problem.

Venues like to 'hike' the bar bill because it is a source of income that cannot be proven, nor denied. Even the till receipts prove nothing because the bar manager can add as many drinks as desired at intervals throughout the event. The only way to reduce (but not eliminate) a nasty shock when the bar bill is presented after the event, is for the event organiser to closely monitor sales *during* the event.

If the guests are to enjoy free drinks at the event and the bar bill will be settled after the event, the budget needs to account for this. It will be an estimated figure, of course, but it must always be an overestimated figure.

6.2.4 Bar vouchers

One effective way of controlling a bar account and preventing it from running wild is to restrict the flow of free drinks. This can be achieved by issuing guests with bar vouchers. It provides the event organiser with a definite amount of credit to be spent at the bar and allows for budget planning. Also, there can be no discrepancy with the venue after the event, because the venue gets paid against the amount of bar vouchers redeemed.

The downside with the bar voucher system is the various prices of drinks – a glass of champagne is not the same price as a pint of beer. Because of this, a venue and the event organiser will agree that bar vouchers are redeemable on certain products only – wine and beers, yes, but not for spirits or premium brands such as cognac and champagne. But guests at events do not like to have their choice restricted, or discover they have ordered something that was not included within their voucher.

From the client point of view, bar vouchers carry a perception to guests that the client is restricting their enjoyment and freedom. Why five vouchers and not ten? And, if the decision was made to provide each guest with five bar vouchers, what happens when they run out?

So, such restraints as a restricted choice of drinks, a guest needing to pay for drinks when the vouchers are spent, and having to pay for some bar products but not others, suggest to the guests that there is some meanness or lack of budget.

Furthermore, it is inconvenient for the venue or event organiser to have to inform guests of the convoluted bar system that has been worked out. Otherwise, it will be an inconvenience for guests to work it out by themselves when they reach the bar and get asked for money. It is ambiguity again, which equates to risk. The risk here is that guests get frustrated or embarrassed at the bar, and this gets converted into dissatisfaction at the event and complaints. The customer experience is compromised.

6.2.5 Credit bars

The most widespread way of providing event guests with free drinks is to agree a limited bar spend with the venue.

How much the limit is will depend on the number of guests and how much it is estimated they will consume during the availability period of drinks – at a conference the bar may be open for only one hour during the break for lunch, for example.

The type of event will need to be considered, as will the profile of guests and the reason for the event. More drinks are consumed at a party than during a conference.

The issue with credit bars is setting the credit limit. And, what happens when the agreed bar spend is reached – should the client up the limit, or will the bar revert to cash? Or, should the bar be free for a restricted time – for the first hour, say?

These are all options to consider. Whichever way it is, the guest at the bar may receive a nasty shock when the bar spend has been reached or the time limit for free drinks has expired and he is asked to open his wallet. This could sour his experience of the event and may result in the client being perceived as penny-pinching.

There is another danger with credit bars: the client may believe the budget for the bar spend is a healthy one and will never be reached. But, it will be surprising how quickly the venue manages to reach that level. When this happens, the client will have no option but to increase the bar budget. Otherwise, the event dries up.

Experience teaches that the best way to navigate the complexity of credit bars – to prevent the venue from overcharging; to provide guests with the best experience without confusion or irritation; and to plan and control the event budget around the bar costs – is to keep it simple and provide an unlimited bar: free drinks throughout the entire event.

Even this, however, will require the event organiser to monitor the bar spend at regular intervals during the event so as to prevent the venue charging whatever the hell they wish when it comes to settling the bill.

It must be arranged for the venue manager or bar manager to regularly report the bar spend to the event organiser – every 30 minutes, say.

This prevents the venue from overloading the bar tab, even if they have enhanced it with a few extra gin and tonics.

It also allows for the venue to seek permission from the event organiser to increase the bar credit limit if required. And it *should* be required. The credit limit should be set at a low level so that it can be increased at intervals with permission of the event organiser. A high bar credit will run out just as quickly as a lower limit. Care should be taken not to inform the venue that there is the possibility to raise the credit limit if necessary. If the venue is aware there is more budget available for the bar, it will always need it.

AUTHOR'S VOICE BOX

During my career in events, I have been an event organiser, bar manager, venue manager and client. In all these roles, I have yet to come across a solution to the great bar argument.

I have reached the conclusion that there are no questions answered with alcohol.

This is especially so when settling the bill on the night of the event and everybody is elated, but exhausted.

Most venues do require the bar bill to be settled on the night, because it will be their experience that clients are lazy when settling accounts after the event has taken place. Besides, if the client is given an opportunity to reflect in the cold light of day on how high the bar spend is . . . Well, that is the starting point of the argument.

This is why it is important to agree the method of bar sales with the venue in advance of the event. And, ensure when doing so that it is measurable, controllable and palatable.

Chapter **7**

Client liaison and communications

7.1 Tickets and invitations

Apart from tickets providing evidence that a guest has paid for access to an event, tickets – and invitations, too – are the mechanisms to ascertain the expected number of guests (or *uptake*). If guests need to purchase a ticket or must respond to an invite in advance of an event, the event organiser gains an idea of how many guests to expect on the day.

RSVP (*Répondez s'il vous plaît*) invitations are not always responded to, it's true, but will still give an indication of how many guests at least intend to attend an event. So it is worthwhile to introduce a reason for people to RSVP – responding gets them a second admission voucher to access the event, a bar voucher to redeem on the day or entry into a prize draw with the admission voucher – these are some ways to encourage RSVPs and get the all-important gauge of uptake.

It should be noted that some guests may not turn up at the event, even if they have requested tickets or responded to the invite. There will likely be a higher rate of *no-shows* if the tickets are free. So, a judgement must be made as to the perceived value of the ticket. The ticket price needs to be at market rate or below, but must also be expensive enough to prevent or reduce drop-off numbers.

For venues, proof of the guest count entering the venue is a legal requirement. This is another reason for producing tickets or invitations – it is vital to understand how many guests are anticipated. Otherwise, too many people could turn up and exceed the venue's legal capacity. This could cause crowd behaviour problems, dangerous overcrowding and the breach of law. It is not overdramatic to state that death can occur in such situations.

Not enough people turning up to an event is also a serious problem. Ticket sales show the uptake. If tickets do not sell, the costs of the event are not covered and it will run at a loss. This is the usual reason events get cancelled at the last minute.

When planning events that are dependent on ticket sales to cover costs and generate profit, it is vital to set a cut-off date. If that number has not been sold by the cut-off date, the event is at risk of bankruptcy and should be cancelled – or at least downscaled to a smaller (and cheaper) venue.

Not knowing how many people are due to attend is a risk brought about by ambiguity. This is not strategic planning: it is chance.

There *must* be a mechanism of knowing numbers of attendees, or at least gaining a realistic expectation of how many guests will attend.

It can thus be identified that the use of tickets is not only for charging admission to an event. Nor is ticketing only a security measure to ensure eligible people enter the event. Tickets also provide a predicted attendance figure and can be collected for an accurate attendance count.

It is worthwhile to issue tickets, even when there is no charge for admission.

7.1.1 Security passes

Tickets, invitations, wristbands and lanyards are issued for security reasons so that people can gain access to the event.

Also, the tickets, invitations, wristbands and lanyards can be colour-coded to differentiate and identify guests. They allow staff and security to distinguish guests from press, VIPs, performers, crew, musicians, entertainers, dancers, caterers etc.

Or, they can be colour-coded to allow the wearer access to restricted areas – white wristbands for balcony seats, gold wristbands for access to the VIP room, red wristbands for backstage access etc.

At most large events, a small poster with all the different types of passes will be displayed at all security checkpoints – the entrance to the venue, entrance to the dressing rooms, entrance to backstage, entrance to production areas, entrance to kitchens, entrance to VIP areas, entrance to crew areas etc. On each poster the passes will be crossed out if those particular passes do not permit access to the entrance where the poster is displayed. So, if all the passes on a poster are crossed out with the exception of VIP passes, only those who wear a VIP pass will be permitted through that particular security checkpoint.

This system enables security personnel to clearly understand and remember which passes are allowed into each area. This is important if security staff get moved about or cover each other for breaks.

The system also provides pictorial confirmation to guests, so that they can see where they are not permitted before approaching security and being denied access. Additionally, by displaying the poster in view of guests, it prevents arguments occurring should a guest feel it is a personal decision being made by a security guard.

At all costs, the access to areas should be clear and transparent. Ambiguity must be avoided, otherwise there is a high risk of arguments and unfairness. The guest should clearly identify their limits of access, and security personnel should not be empowered with the decision of which guest goes where.

7.1.1.1 Access All Areas passes

If the event dictates a need for a range of passes, there is also a requirement for one single pass that permits access to everywhere within the venue without restriction. This is known as the Access All Areas or 'Triple A' pass.

The AAA pass is for top-level, key management personnel and would be limited in number and distribution.

A person wearing an AAA pass will not be challenged by security.

The small poster of passes at security checkpoints will still show the AAA pass as an example to security personnel. It is another example of not allowing ambiguity into the system. However, the AAA pass on the poster would not be crossed out because the privileged wearer has Access All Areas.

7.1.2 Invitations

Traditionally, invitations get mailed four weeks prior to an event. But this does vary, especially with reliance on invites via email and social media. The advance period is to allow attendees to insert the date in their diary in good time.

If invitations are late, the more likely people's diaries will be committed to other engagements.

When diary dates are filled, it is a difficult task to clear the date in order to attend the event. Besides, VIPs and busy guests may not attend because they will not cancel a previously scheduled obligation.

Often, a follow-up invitation is mailed seven to ten days prior to the event, as a reminder.

The need for passes, invitations, wristbands, lanyards or tickets must be ascertained at the brief, so as to build the cost of print and production into the budget. This is another variable cost that is dependent on the number of guests, but if the attendance is high, so this cost will be too.

7.2 Client liaison

When the event organiser receives the brief from the client, there can be a period of quiet research during which time the proposal and proposed budget are being constructed.

However, once the client accepts and agrees the proposal, ongoing liaison between the event organiser and the client is crucial.

The event organiser/client relationship is a dual one. Even so, the event organiser is responsible for this because the client is busy on other things and many things.

The event organiser must consistently feed information to the client. This builds the client relationship, both professionally and personally.

People like to work with people they like.

The best clients – and an event organiser wants all clients to be their best clients – are those which are liked. Likeability develops through contact, communication and the evolvement of a relationship.

Good liaison allows the client access to decisions and issues. It would be bad practice to make a wrong decision on behalf of the client, or for the client to disagree with a decision that has already been made, or for the client to belatedly be informed about an issue that has grown out of the event organiser's control.

For larger events, regular client meetings can be diarised – once-weekly or once-monthly.

But, time passes quickly – especially when an event organiser is multitasking on a number of projects. So, even for smaller events it is worthwhile getting regular client meetings into the diary.

The event organiser needs to maintain liaison with the client at a level that eliminates any potential for surprise.

Every twist, turn and change of direction that occurs must be shared between the event organiser and the client.

The level of communication is the difference between great success and small failure.

7.3 Event checklist

The client file will be being built during the period of planning and organising, which will usually be for no less than three months, but can be up to eighteen months or possibly even longer. Contracts and orders from suppliers will be filling the file. Notes from client conversations and meetings will be generated. Venue visits with suppliers will be recorded . . .

Because of the lead-in period and the range of elements needed to make an event happen, the event organiser should keep an event checklist at the front of each client file.

There is an example event checklist in Appendix III.

The event checklist is a document that is gradually completed during the pre-event planning. It helps to ensure no requirement gets overlooked during the planning, which is an extended period and can overlap with the planning and execution of other event jobs.

It is necessary to rigidly *maintain* the event checklist during the pre-event planning, so as to highlight elements of the event that are completed, and those that remain outstanding.

7.4 Administration checklist

The administration checklist is a reminder of which documents have been completed during the lead-in, and which are outstanding.

There is an example administration checklist in Appendix IV.

This checklist helps ensure the order and sequence of documentation, and reminds an event organiser of payment-due dates.

7.5 Production companies

Production companies provide technical aspects for events, although some event companies do production and some production companies do event management.

If a production company is being used to 'produce the show', they will be in liaison with the event organiser and will probably visit the venue each time the event organiser does.

As with all suppliers, no meetings should happen at the venue without the event organiser being present. This must be made known to new suppliers and reinforced to previous or existing suppliers.

It is essential for the event organiser to maintain control. Splinter meetings that exclude the event organiser will dilute control.

The production manager is effectively the deputy event organiser and is responsible for all technical requirements that the event demands, such as sound, lighting, audio visual, projection, stage design, stage build, creative technical elements (pyrotechnics, snow machines, fog machines, confetti cannons), running the show and managing the technical crew. Anything that is operated technically is the responsibility of the production manager.

The event organiser will be working alongside on all other aspects of the event and *overseeing* the technical elements as one aspect of the entire event.

It is important to recognise that the production manager and event organiser work alongside each other and support each other. These are not two roles that come together for the event: they travel alongside each other.

7.5.1 Show producer

The producer can be provided by the production company, or this can be a freelance specialist.

The producer will provide the running order (sometimes called the *technical schedule* or *technical rider*) for the show, including fashion shows.

A producer will *call* the show (production managers are often referred to as *show-callers*) to their production crew by means of a headset microphone system known as *talk-back*. The headsets are referred to as *cans*.

During the show, the entire production crew will maintain silence, except to acknowledge the caller's instructions and standby alerts.

Typically, what can be heard over the cans is: 'Cue intro music; lights stand by; lights go . . .'

Show-calling is a skill. Nothing must happen on stage without it being 'called' first by the show-caller.

AUTHOR'S VOICE BOX

To highlight the need for professional show-calling and production crew, there was an incident at a celebrity-packed catwalk show during London Fashion Week.

One of the world's top supermodels was instructed to exit the stage at the front of the catwalk where she would meet a security guard and be escorted through the audience to get backstage.

As soon as she stepped off the stage, a lift in the centre of the stage would then drop 25 ft into the basement, ready for another supermodel to step onto the lift and appear in front of the audience and press.

On the night of the fashion show, the first model strutted to the front of the catwalk, as planned. The lift dropped 25 ft into the basement.

But, the model then turned and walked *back* along the catwalk towards the gaping hole!

It is unknown whether the show-caller was at fault for calling for the lift to drop too soon, before the model had stepped off the catwalk. Or it could have been the lift operator who perhaps anticipated the instruction and pressed the 'down' button too soon. It might have been the model's error for forgetting the instruction to exit the catwalk and not turn around and walk back onto the stage – or she may not even have been given that instruction.

Whatever did happen, that lift should never have dropped while the model was still on-stage. Such an error could have had serious consequences – injury or death.

It demonstrates the need for a show-caller, and the need for the crew to act only upon instruction.

Fortunately, on this occasion the world's most famous supermodel did not plummet to serious injury or death. Disaster was averted by the quick reaction of the supermodel herself. She spotted the gaping chasm in front of her and clambered around the scenery to get off the stage.

Next morning, the press misinterpreted the situation and reported how the model had stormed from the stage in a melodramatic tantrum fit for a diva. But, the headlines *could* have been far worse than that.

It can now be understood why an event organiser is not an event producer. Production is a specialism which an event organiser may or may not possess. In any case, the event organiser is required to oversee all elements of the event, and cannot be restricted to the production box for the entirety of the show.

• • •

By now, it can be seen how the job of an event organiser is to weave and stitch each element together *before* the event takes place. It is precision planning, liaison, communication and detail. It is the exclusion of risk. This mighty effort happens *pre*-event.

There exists a perception that the role of organising events is exciting and glamorous, and that it is only about mixing with the stars. But, the stars at an event are also guests, who have their expectations to be fulfilled, too. Whether it is a client, a guest or a supermodel, event management is work. No matter who it is in the room, the event organiser will be thinking about lighting levels, the music and whether the canapés are hot enough.

In reality, the 'fun' of being an event organiser to the stars comes when talking about it afterwards.

Other than the crew and event team, no-one sees the extent of the research, the preparations, the production meetings, the venue visits on rainy Tuesday afternoons . . .

The reason the job of an event organiser is perceived to be glamorous is because people only see the glitz on the night. For them to see that side only is the event organiser's job.

The part that guests see is the section of event management that is the 'middle' section, as it were. This is the section that comes next.

PART 3

Management on-site: operational event management

Chapter

Event organiser responsibilities

On-site event management – that is to say, event management at the venue on the day of a live happening – is a marked difference from the research, planning, administration and meticulous detailing that are required pre-event.

Now, the event organiser becomes *operational*.

Whereas pre-event planning was predominantly desk-based, when the event organiser moves into operational management, the role demands team leadership, management, delegation and communication.

And, where planning is proactive – forecasting requirements, issues and thinking ahead about safety – operational management can trick an event organiser into reactive management.

The event organiser must also demonstrate professionalism and instil confidence. And, whilst performing all these skills and functions, the client is now alongside to observe and interject.

On-site event management is about dealing with logistics and people.

It means being friendly with everyone. And, being friends with no-one. It is about losing oneself in a Bermuda triangle of working in a social environment, ensuring everybody else is having a good time, and managing to retain professionalism in all circumstances. It is always being on duty.

Alcohol, sociality and events go together, and too many times an event organiser gets caught on one side of the triangle or another, while not maintaining an anchored position between being social, ensuring others are enjoying themselves, and retaining professionalism. Often, an event organiser can be seen standing and chatting with the client with a glass of champagne in their hand, or standing at the buffet and gnawing at chicken wings. This is not good management; it is called having a good time, which is not why the event organiser is there.

Only when the last guest has left the venue can the event organiser begin to relax. Even then, however, it is not over until the client has left, too. After that, there is the venue get-out (*de-rig* or *break-down*) to execute, which is a potentially dangerous part of the event because what took care and precision to install and erect before the event, is now waste and can be torn down as quickly as possible. There are a lot of people involved with the break-down and care gets forgotten. Elements that were rigged overhead are now being uncoupled. Lighting and sound stacks are being dismantled. A sense of anti-climax is felt: the job is done. The crew will be tired; it will be late; and they want to get home.

Truly, the event organiser is on duty until leaving the venue himself. If a situation were to arise or an accident occur, the event organiser must be present . . . and *must* be sober.

But, that is the de-rig stage after the event. During the event, the event organiser must be overseeing and supervising, and must be available, wherever required. The event organiser must be mobile. Event management is not an office job. Before the event gets going, the event organiser is checking.

8.1 Checking

With the event in build stage on the day, the job of the event organiser is *checking*.

The event organiser will *check* that everything that was planned so meticulously is now happening.

Checking the correct number of chairs and tables are delivered; checking the branding is on-site; checking the branding is in place; checking the production manager is contented; checking the flowers have been delivered; checking the entertainment has arrived and is setting up . . .

Every element of the event must be checked.

One of the key elements is to check the client is satisfied. This is a constant check throughout the day of the event. But, this does not mean having to ask the client to establish their satisfaction – this would get annoying. Watching the client from a distance and checking how they are interacting with their guests is enough to ascertain their level of satisfaction with how the event is going.

Watching the client and letting them see that they are being watched is another demonstration of the event organiser's attention to detail and care to ensure the client is happy. It lets a client know they are important and valued.

Additionally, watching a client allows the event organiser to pre-empt their needs – if their glass is empty, say, or if the client is looking around for the event organiser.

Checking and rechecking is the main activity of the event organiser's day.

When the doors open, the entrance procedures (security, VIP lists, door hosts, registration, reception, cloakroom) are being checked. When the food is being served, the waiters are being checked; the kitchen is checked; the service is being checked.

It is not enough for the event organiser to ask for something to be done. It must be checked that whatever it was *did* get done. Nothing is left to assumption. The art of the job is to minimise risk. This includes the risk of things not getting done, even after asking for them. It needs checking.

8.2 Hosting

Once the venue opens to guests the event organiser's role transforms into that of a host.

It begins at the front door – as guests arrive at the event.

The event organiser will be positioned at the front door to check that the flow of guests and the entry procedures are working effectively. This is the area of immediate concern because this is where the action begins and there is a lot happening – guest lists to check, security, VIP arrivals, press and paparazzi, registration, checking tickets, invitations, bracelets or lanyards.

All this needs executing professionally, efficiently, quickly and courteously.

Problems must be quickly identified and must be rectified, such as guests arriving without tickets.

After the front door, the cloakroom is the next area to check. Then it will be the bar to check the service. Then, a visit to the production office to check the production manager is ready, and so on.

The event organiser may assist staff, but must also oversee; he must 'float'.

If staff require physical assistance – in the cloakroom, say – the event organiser will identify the problem and bring additional staff from other areas to alleviate the problem. It is a good idea to bring a waiter to help in the cloakroom because waiters are not serving food at the very beginning of an event.

'Floating' means that the event organiser can oversee all areas and make adjustments where necessary. This approach allows the delegation of duties among the team and shifting staff to the busiest areas. It is flexibility that is key. It can be seen how operational event management is reactive: reacting to the immediate needs and demands of the event as it unfolds.

But, the event organiser will not take any task upon himself; he must be able to remove himself easily.

Management is absolutely not about becoming a unit of labour. It is not for the event organiser to be serving behind the bar, or taking coats at the cloakroom. Labour is what the staff are employed to do. The production crew are responsible for the stage; the security guards are trained for crowd safety; the waiting staff know very well how to serve the food . . .

It is acceptable for the event organiser to temporarily assist to alleviate a situation. This would be expected by the staff and the client. An event organiser cannot stand by and watch a situation. But, the assistance must not interrupt the duty of overseeing all aspects of the event. This is important because when it comes to the evaluation procedures post-event, the event organiser must know what happened. This is especially necessary if the client is unhappy with any aspect of the event.

The event organiser is responsible for having the people there on the day to do the job, ensuring that they know what to do and how to do it, and that they have the resources to do so. After this, it only requires checking.

Operational event management is about checking, re-checking and overseeing. It is ensuring that what was planned for is happening.

Now that it is understood how an event organiser must perform, we can look in detail at the sequence of on-site event management on the day of the event.

8.3 The running order

The running order (*on-site schedule*, or *function sheet*) is a timeline of activities that are planned to happen on the day of the event from start to finish: from venue get-in to venue get-out.

There is an example running order in Appendix V.

The purpose of this vital document is to inform every person working at the event of what is happening, when it should happen and who is responsible for doing it.

The running order is distributed prior to the day of the event to the management team (production manager, catering manager, venue manager, security, key suppliers and the client).

The reason for early distribution of the running order is so that key personnel can acquaint themselves with the planned details in advance of the event. These specialists may review the information at leisure and might suggest adjustments, in which case the event organiser would make modifications to the running order and redistribute a second edition.

Although the key personnel require the running order in advance, the timing of distribution needs to be close enough to the date of the event that all details are known and few, if any, additions would be required.

For large or complex events, the management team would have a pre-event briefing meeting where the running order is distributed and discussed.

The exact format of the running order differs from event organiser to event organiser.

AUTHOR'S VOICE BOX

I prefer *not* to publish a contact list on the running order because of the risk of it falling into the wrong hands – even the hands of the venue or my client. I do not wish to provide anybody with a ready-made list of my trusted suppliers that took years to evolve and which they would receive in the one document.

Instead, I keep my contact list securely in the client file for my use, and publish only my details on the front of the running order so that I am contactable to relay information or answer questions.

Sometimes, I will publish the venue contact details in the running order for logistical reasons, such as deliveries and access – but venue information is not personal or sensitive because it is available and easy to obtain, anyhow.

It is not unusual for the event organiser to attach a contact list of key personnel involved with the event, including suppliers and organisations, and their mobile numbers and email addresses. If this is needed, it is advisable to print that contact list on the first page of the running order and distribute this page to the top management team only. This is because of the sensitivity of the personal contact information. Copies of the running order will get left behind after the event by all departments and will turn up backstage, in the cloakroom, in the kitchen, behind the reception desk, in bins and on the floor.

The running order begins by listing the first activity to happen on the day (or set-up days if there are any). Usually, the first activity is the get-in. The last activity will be the get-out which is when the venue must be cleared (including break-down days if there are any).

Between the get-in and the get-out, the running order lists every activity planned to happen on the day of the event in time-order.

With the page divided into three columns, the left column lists the timing of each activity. The centre column lists the detail of each activity. The right column lists who is responsible for each activity.

A fourth column may be added for the event organiser to tick when each activity has been checked and has happened (see Table 2).

The running order can also be used for making notes during the progression of the event. Notes can include instances where timings changed – due to overruns of presentations, say, and this impacted on the late service of catering. The document therefore provides a written reflection of what *actually* happened during the event which is helpful when conducting post-event evaluation.

Every person who is working the event must follow the running order, and because everything within it has been planned, there should be no reason for deviation. This is why the running order is one of the last documents to be produced prior to the event, when all details are known and are set. It is common practice, however, for the event organiser to build the running order during the lead-in planning stages. Information can be added in an ongoing fashion so that

Table 2 Example running order (fragment)

Timing	Activity	Who	Checked
08:30	Client on-site	Organiser	
09:00	Stage ready	Production	
09:15–09:30	Sound check	Production	
09:15	Decoration begins	Decorator	

the running order provides a picture of the day of the event. However, the finished running order will not be produced until all elements are known and fixed.

The technical manager (production manager) may produce a technical running order for the running of the stage show or presentation. This would be distributed to the technical crew only and the 'activities' would be their stage directions.

8.4 Sequence

On the day of an event there is a natural sequence. This will vary from event to event, but an experienced event organiser will become familiar with the natural sequence of an event day.

Although it is a 'natural' sequence, it must be carefully planned and then managed. Otherwise, the sequence will turn into a mess and then things will run out of sequence.

Typically, the sequence runs as follows:

1   Get-in

   – Access to the venue

   – Deliveries

2   Tables and chairs set in place (ready for the light focusing or *spotting*)

3   Set-up

   – Stage build

   – Light installation, rigging and focusing

   – Projection installation

   – Sound installation and check

4   Decoration begins

5   Crew lunch

6   Rehearsal

7   Tables laid (when the waiters arrive on-site)

8   Decoration finished

9   Staff briefing

10   Final venue check

11   Doors open.

It is important for the natural sequence to be planned because not everybody can perform their role at the same time in a venue. The tables have to be set up before the waiters can lay them, for example. So, each activity must be thought through and planned, and the teams must be allocated their timings.

It would be costly to bring the waiters on-site three hours before they can lay the tables. This is why the running order is so important for everybody working the event: it informs who needs to be where, when and what for.

When an event begins in the morning or afternoon, the requirements will be set in place in the venue the day before or overnight. This is because there would be no time to do the build in the morning before guests arrived.

Only for events that open in the evening onwards – when there is time before guests arrive – is the build done on the day of the event.

Depending on the complexity, the build may not need to take an entire day on the day before. It could be an afternoon build, an evening build or an overnight build.

Whatever the duration of a build the day before an event, a venue would normally charge half of their daily hire rate.

For the purpose of example, this book assumes it is a daytime build on the day of an evening event.

The technical build receives early priority because sets, staging, and sound and lighting take time to construct and rig. Often, the technical manager will begin setting up before the arrival of the event organiser. This is accepted practice because these two key managers would have planned everything beforehand. Besides, the event organiser is not expected to get involved with the production build – it is a tech crew job.

8.5 Production office

When the event organiser arrives on-site, the first activity would be to establish the production office: the event base from where the event is run.

This is a key first duty so that subsequent personnel have an office base where they can source resources, report in, collect handheld radios, store their belongings and pass on communications.

The production office may also be the base for the security team, the staff sign-in and sign-out, and an office manager.

Usually, the on-site production office will be an office or meeting room provided by the venue. Or, if the event is on a green-field site, the production office might be a caravan, trailer, portable cabin or small marquee.

It will need to be large enough to accommodate all requirements and will possibly double up as storage space for supplies and uniforms. Otherwise, separate secure and lockable storage facilities will be required (especially for storing coveted commodities, such as alcohol). Because the production office will be staffed by a trusted team member, it would be an unnecessary expense to procure separate storage facilities.

The production office must be staffed at all times, because staff, suppliers and contractors will report to this office when they arrive on-site. Usually, one member of the event team will be assigned to remain in the production office for the duration of the event, including the set-up and de-rig. Planning documents and the client file will be kept in the production office for reference, as will a 'field kit' that contains necessary equipment such as torches and a first-aid kit.

AUTHOR'S VOICE BOX

A high-profile event was organised to recognise notable women.

It was held in a reputable business venue in the heart of a European capital city.

Seated in the audience as a guest, it took just a few minutes for me to realise the event had not been rehearsed.

The well-dressed women speakers were not shown how to get on stage, nor where to exit. However well-attired they appeared, they also appeared stupid. The audience laughed and those on stage were embarrassed.

They were not coached on how to hold a microphone or how to turn it on. They didn't know where to sit. And, one poor speaker – a very recognisable actress – did not even know she was there to speak – she thought she was there was an invited guest!

My regret was that I could not record the event to teach the effects of not rehearsing an event.

I insist my clients must rehearse if they wish to make a speech. If the CEO of a company does not have time to rehearse, he does not go on my stage. I simply will not risk embarrassing him to his audience.

If global music stars such as Rihanna, Justin Bieber and U2 can make time to rehearse, so can a company CEO.

The event organiser may be based in the production office, but would not be the one whose duty it is to remain in the office. If the event organiser is tempted to stay in the office because it is the hub for communication, handheld radios will be the solution to enable him to get out and 'float'.

8.6 Rehearsal

It is also vital for the technical requirements to be complete before the rehearsal can take place. Rehearsals are essential. Even if it is a simple presentation or speech by one person it must be rehearsed. Nobody must present an award or make a presentation if they have not rehearsed.

If there is a stage, there is a rehearsal.

The above simple rule must not be broken. Ever.

Because of time constraints and the hectic schedule of building an event on the day, the rehearsal often gets squeezed out of the sequence. This is especially so when things are running late or the production crew are under pressure to get ready before the doors open so they concede to forgo the rehearsal. This is dangerous: it is risk.

The rehearsal time will be on the running order, so even if the timings go awry, it is not acceptable to omit an activity that is important enough to be on the running order.

The problem is that the 'doors open' time takes precedence over everything else, including the rehearsal. That time of opening doors draws close and quickly. Activities that have not been achieved before that all-important time of doors opening get squeezed out. But, it is not a law that the doors must open on time – it can be done late for the sake of getting the event right and making it safe.

Even if a technical rehearsal does happen for the benefit of the crew to practise their directions, it is essential to rehearse the presenters or speakers as well – and *this* is the bit that often gets squeezed out.

It is unprofessional to humiliate someone in front of an audience because there was no rehearsal.

Often, it is the speaker herself who feels she need not rehearse. But, if somebody does not rehearse, they should not be on the stage. Every professional artist or presenter rehearses, and so must keynote speakers and company CEOs. A speaker needs to hear her voice through the sound system; she needs to know where to access the stage and where to exit; she needs to know where to stand.

The presenters should arrive early to rehearse before the event opens to guests. If the guests are attending an arrival reception in another space, the presenters can be taken to the main room for a short rehearsal whilst the reception is in progress.

8.7 Caterers

The caterer (if not in-house) will require an early get-in, so as to set up their kitchen and equipment.

If the menu is hot food, cooking time will impact the preparation time. Less time would be required for cold buffet or canapé menus. There will also be less furniture to set up and lay for canapés and buffets. Even so, the catering team is always one of the earliest on-site.

Apart from equipment which may or may not be required by the caterer, they will need space. An event caterer will need to lay out plates of food for preparation and decoration. Lack of space is the enemy for event catering.

If the venue is supplying furniture, it would probably already be in place. Otherwise, the caterer's porters will set up the tables before the waiters arrive in the late afternoon to lay the cutlery and glassware. Sometimes, the porters will lay the tables before the waiters arrive.

The key issue is to minimise the cost of labour because waiters are paid by the hour (*casual staff*). Also, it is not good practice to have a team of bored casual staff hanging around the venue with nothing to do – it is demotivating as well as costly.

Laying the tables can take place during the afternoon because it will not interfere with other activities, such as setting up the stage. However, the tables may need to be in position early (even if they are not laid) to establish the layout of the space, to judge sightlines for the stage, calculate timings for presenters or awards recipients to walk to the stage, divide the waiter stations, and other logistics.

The lighting engineer may require the tables to be in position for the accurate positioning of spotlights onto the dining tables (referred to as *focusing* or *spotting* the lights). This activity can take a long time. Additionally, the follow-spot operators will need to rehearse their role of tracking awards recipients from their seat in the audience to the stage.

The decoration team or the florist may require the tables to be in place for them to work on the table-centres. Table-centre features should be designed to ensure the decoration does not obstruct guests from seeing each other across the table, or from seeing the stage. For this reason, table-centre decorations should be built low, or placed on high pedestals.

The use of candles and naked flames for aesthetic purposes on tables should be avoided because they are potential fire risks due to scarves and long hair.

8.8 Theme and decoration

Theme and decoration takes place during the day, whilst the stage build is happening and the furniture is being positioned, because decoration time can be extensive and will not interfere with other activities.

It is quite usual for rehearsals to commence whilst tables are being laid and decorated.

8.9 Entertainment riders

If there is an appearance by a professional, this is called *talent* and can be a host, presenter, speaker, musician, singer, band, performer, act, DJ, entertainer, comedian or celebrity.

Professional talent will be booked through, and represented by, a talent agent.

The talent's representative will provide the event organiser with a rider (also known as an *entertainment rider* or *artist rider*).

The rider is a document that stipulates the needs and requirements of the talent. It also forms the booking contract.

Therefore, it is wise for the event organiser to request the talent's rider *before* confirming the booking of talent because some of the requirements may be too costly for the event budget to sustain. Or it might be impossible to fulfil the rider because of the venue's limitations. Or, the requirements in the rider may simply be unjustifiable.

By way of example, some riders stipulate dressing rooms must be within a certain distance of the stage, must be a certain size, with a shower and separate toilet, a window that opens and a view of the Eiffel Tower. In small London theatres, this is not possible to achieve.

It is well known that riders can be wild and eccentric. Some celebrities refuse to share dressing rooms. Others stipulate a particular brand of bottled water at a certain temperature. But, there is a serious side to riders because technical requirements of the artist are stipulated. These may be preferences or they could be because the artist is contractually obligated – it may be that a pianist is contracted to only perform in public on a Yamaha piano, for example.

The cost of booking talent or a celebrity is the *appearance fee* for their attendance or performance. The costs of providing the requirements on their rider are additional and borne by the client, which means they come from the event budget.

8.10 Staff briefing

All staff who are working at the event must be briefed to receive information on the key elements.

Most of the event team – many of whom would have event management experience – will have deduced a clear understanding of the event from the running order, pre-event correspondence, pre-event meetings and from working alongside the event organiser on-site when a lot of information gets picked up.

However, a proportion of the staff will be introduced to the event on the day – particularly casual staff such as bar and waiting staff. So, it is necessary for the event organiser to consider this and convey key information, such as the reason for the event, who are the VIPs attending, who the client is and an overview of the running order.

The event organiser should plan what information the staff need if a guest were to ask them questions: when the doors open; what time the bar closes; and where the toilets are.

Some event organisers do the staff briefing in departmental groups as the staff arrive on-site for duty. Others brief the entire staff team once they are all on-site.

The latter option is beneficial for ensuring each staff member understands another member of staff's role and the pressure they may be under. It is also a better option if there is a likelihood of changing staff roles during the event – taking a waiter off the floor to assist in the cloakroom, for example. In such a situation, it is useful if all staff were present at the one briefing.

Also, on a busy and tight schedule – which event days always are – it can be advantageous to have just one briefing meeting taking place. It saves time. And, it saves the event organiser from having to repeat instructions to various departments, or risk missing some piece of information by changing the message to suit the waiters, or the bar staff, say.

Additionally, if a staff member raises a question during the briefing meeting, it could be important for all other staff to hear the answer.

Finally, it can be important to have all the staff together for the briefing so as to introduce key personnel, such as the head of security, the sponsor or the client.

Certainly, one briefing meeting for all staff is easier to schedule onto the running order so that everyone knows when it is happening.

The event organiser will conduct the briefing because this is the one person who possesses all information about all areas. It is also an opportunity for the event organiser to make themselves known to staff and instil authority, leadership and confidence.

The client may attend the briefing, but should at least be pointed out to the staff.

Keep the brief brief.

The brief for staff should be just that: brief. It should ideally take about ten minutes, and not longer than 15 to 20 minutes.

It should ideally take place between 30 – 45 minutes before the doors open. This is when everything is in place, all staff are on-site, nothing is likely to change, the staff will remember the information and most of their setting up will be complete, with just minor jobs to do before the doors open.

If the briefing is kept to ten minutes, there will be time before the doors open for the event organiser to conduct a final walk-round of the venue.

However, if time is short at this critical point, the staff briefing must still happen. It is on the running order and it is one of the procedures of event management so it cannot get pushed out because of timing issues.

It would be better to open the doors late than to not brief the staff. And, with the final venue walk-round still to happen, the doors may have to open late because the final check is another important and necessary procedure (see 8.14).

Catering and waiting staff are sometimes briefed *additionally* by the catering manager, so that their roles can be discussed in specific detail including the menu they will be serving. This is particularly the case for banquets where formal service is strictly managed.

Security personnel should receive a specific briefing. This is because security details may be confidential, or because the general staff do not need to be delayed in setting up by hearing about security information.

8.11 Pre-event briefing

Pre-event briefing is when the briefing meeting takes place before the day of the event.

This can be because key staff, such as the management team, are available as a cohort to be briefed pre-event in readiness for the event day. The benefit of this is in briefing key personnel without the time limitations, time restrictions, time pressures, the presence of multitasking and distractions.

Where an event is happening all day or from early morning, a pre-event briefing is more appropriate. It is also not unusual to hold a pre-event briefing day for volunteer staff where it is important to give information before the event day, and would not incur wage costs for volunteers to attend the briefing.

8.12 On-site briefing

An on-site briefing happens at the venue on the day of the event.

This is the only option when briefing casual staff and venue staff who are working the event on the day. It would be neither feasible nor cost-effective to call them all in for a briefing meeting before they are there on the day of the event.

Note: It is not uncommon for an event organiser to schedule a pre-event briefing for managers and key staff, *and* an on-site briefing for casual staff or to update on last-minute details or changes.

8.13 Security

Venues provide security because their security staff are licensed and know the idiosyncrasies of the venue. They also know the faces of local people, which can sometimes be helpful.

Otherwise, the event organiser will hire security from a reputable security provider.

Even where security is provided by the venue, an event organiser may decide to hire additional security. This could be to maintain control of all elements of the event. Security staff being known to the event organiser enables control over their actions. Otherwise, the event organiser would be handing control of security over to the venue. It is also important that the event organiser gives security the instruction to open doors when ready to do so. It must not be that the venue, or security themselves, open the doors and allow guests into the venue just because the clock says it is the right time (see 8.14).

Security is not only required at the front door. It is also necessary for safety, crowd management, crowd control and to control sensitive areas inside the venue. Security may be needed to prevent the audience invading the stage (crowd management means the procedures put in place to manage crowds, whereas crowd control means measures to bring a crowd back into control).

VIPs may require security whilst walking through the venue. If there is a VIP area, the entrance to this will require security.

AUTHOR'S VOICE BOX

I was managing a private VIP party in the function suite of a smart boutique hotel.

All drinks were free to invited guests.

The hotel provided security, but I took additional security because I did not know the venue and was concerned about handing control over to their security team.

During the evening, the number of guests surpassed the invited quota and it was noticeable that some guests did not fit the profile of the event.

It transpired that the hotel's security staff allowed their friends in to enjoy the free bar and mingle with VIPs.

I was pleased to have my trusted security personnel on-site to stem the tide of unauthorised guests.

Security should be posted at each entrance to dressing rooms, backstage areas, press rooms, VIP areas and hospitality areas. At each checkpoint there will be a poster showing pictures of the full range of tickets, passes, lanyards or wristbands, with those ones crossed out that do not permit the holder access to that particular area.

8.13.1 Handheld radios

Under the remit of security and good communication among the key team, the need for hiring radio handsets should be considered.

In a busy venue or a sizeable area, communication between departments and the event management team is essential.

8.14 Final walk-round

Before the event organiser gives security the go-ahead to open the doors and allow guests into the venue, a final walk-round of the venue should be undertaken.

This is the final opportunity for the event organiser to check everything is in place. But, safety is the main purpose of the final walk-round.

A final venue walk-round should take no longer than 10 to 15 minutes. It is scheduled onto the running order as the last activity before doors open.

The final walk-round takes the event organiser to every corner of the venue to check every area is ready to accept guests.

The watchword here is 'check'. Whenever a staff member is asked to do something, the event organiser must always check it has been done. The 10 or 15 minutes it takes to walk round the venue is the final chance to check.

If the event is in a venue, the venue manager should accompany the event organiser so that any outstanding issues can be dealt with speedily.

If the final walk-round identifies a problem or an area that is not ready, the doors cannot open until the situation has been resolved – even if it means delaying guests outside the venue.

This may seem extreme and unprofessional, but it is the event organiser's duty and responsibility to ensure every area of the venue is ready – and safe – before guests enter the area.

This is as much for fire, health and safety reasons as it is for presentation. Events are temporary and they require temporary installations. Temporary means risk.

Common issues to be identified during the final venue walk-round are as follows:

- Trip hazards: cables laid across dark carpets must be covered; temporary carpeting curling at the edges must be taped down; the extended feet of tripods supporting speakers or lights must be roped off or highlighted with hazard tape.

- Fire-fighting equipment: extinguishers may have been removed during the set-up – to hold doors open, for instance. They must be retrieved and replaced.

- Emergency exits: escape routes must be free of obstructions. This occurs when deliveries, boxes, stored items or spare furniture are temporarily stored in corridors and escape routes. Exits and escape routes can also get blocked by pop-up banners, branding and stands being positioned in areas that are required to be kept free by law.

- Emergency signage: emergency lighting and signage can become obscured by temporary branding or pop-up banners, drapes, curtaining, flowers and decorations.

- Fire doors: fire exit doors must be unlocked before the venue allows guests inside. A detail such as this can be overlooked with the bustling nature of

AUTHOR'S VOICE BOX

At a show during London Fashion Week, the stage backdrop was a floor-to-ceiling mirror.

For safety and ease of transport the designer's production manager had specified a lightweight material with a mirrored surface.

However, only glass provides a reflection without distortion.

So, when the models rehearsed (another benefit of rehearsing), it looked like they were in the Funny Maze of Mirrors at a funfair.

At the last minute, it was decided to replace the backdrop with a huge glass mirror. This had to be sourced, delivered and installed before the guests could be allowed into the venue. It caused the doors to open *two hours* late, and guests such as Boy George and Mick Jagger were kept waiting outside until the event organiser gave the instruction for security to open the doors.

This is an extreme example. But, it does demonstrate the need for the venue to be ready before guests are granted access, regardless of the time printed on the ticket or invitation. Control is imperative. It is not law that the doors must open on time.

• • •

On another occasion – an awards banquet for 2,000 guests at a hotel on Park Lane – I was dissatisfied with one element of the preparations and delayed the opening by just 15 minutes.

The sponsor was furious and insisted that I open the doors. I refused. It had to be my decision, not his.

Always ask – *who is the real event manager?*

• • •

By insisting doors do not open until I give the go-ahead, I have realised there is a benefit: it works for creating a buzz outside the doors.

It is sometimes a problem to admit the first early guests who wander around an empty venue. It can be better to open the doors just a little late, waiting until a small throng of guests are excitedly waiting to flow through the doors.

Care must be taken not to upset guests by keeping them waiting too long. But, when judged correctly, it can be a positive aspect to open the doors a little late.

temporary events taking place and being set up. Fire-retaining doors must be closed and not blocked from automatic closing.

- White tape should be applied to mark visible edges, steps, stage edges, trip hazards, tripod legs and other hazards. Routes backstage from dressing rooms to the stage should be clearly marked with white tape. This is another reason why the final walk-round is done last thing – so that the lights are set ready for opening and such hazards can now be identified.

Venue managers panic when the time to open the doors arrives and guests are gathering outside. The venue will want the doors to be opened on time. But, the event organiser must remain in control. If the final walk-round has not yet been undertaken, or there is an issue that was identified during the walk-round and still has to be resolved (the event organiser must revisit areas where there were issues, to be assured they are now rectified), the doors must remain closed. This is why it is worthwhile for the event organiser to have security under control, so as not to allow the venue manager to instruct security to open the doors.

8.15 Fire, health and safety

When planning an event, the fire, health and safety (FH&S) implications must be considered and planned, also.

It would be too late to begin considering these essential elements on-site because the safety aspects need to have already been identified and addressed so that the necessary measures are in place on the day.

It is even too late to begin thinking about safety halfway through the planning process, because the proposal and budget will need to reflect safety implications and associated costs. These types of costs may include marshals, medics, lifeguards, lifeboat and crew, fire marshals, ambulance, first-aid provision, first-aid point, crowd barriers and safety notices.

If the brief is for a conference, the implications and costs would be negligible. But, if the requirement is for a circus theme with acrobats, high trapezes and fire-eaters, there will be implications to plan for and pay for.

Health and safety can sometimes be approached as a laborious task. At best, it can sometimes be seen as an additional task after all the creative and fun stuff has been taken care of.

But, as important as each element of an event is to the professional and dedicated event organiser, it is obvious that safety cannot be compromised. Health and Safety is not difficult. Actually, it can be extremely interesting – after all, it is about safeguarding yourself, your staff and your guests.

8.15.1 Risk assessment

Conducting a risk assessment for the event will identify any FH&S issues as part of the event management process. It is also a legal requirement for most events. At least, it is good and essential practice to conduct a risk assessment for every event.

While assessing the risks, identified risks are graded as to the severity of harm they would cause and the likelihood of them occurring.

After this, measures must be put in place to minimise or eliminate those risks and ensure the safety of all event stakeholders (see Figure 3).

Risks at events can include:

- Crowd behaviour due to young age, drugs or alcohol. These are known as 'unintended social consequences'.

    - Prevention: search attendees, ensure sufficient stewards, first-aid on-site.

- Temporary carpeting laid but not secured.

    - Prevention: secure all carpets with edging and tape, ensure good lighting, highlight edges.

- Cables stretched across floors and carpets.

    - Prevention: run cables along walls or up and around doorways, cover or tape over the cables, use coloured cables, do not lay dark cables over dark carpets.

- Obstructed fire escape routes.

Figure 3 Risk assessment process

- Prevention: ensure a check is in place to keep escape routes clear.

- Children's activities.

  - Prevention: ensure sufficient supervision, first-aid on-site.

- Presence of water.

  - Prevention: lifebelts, lifeguards, lifeboat and crew, warning notices, fencing or barriers, provision of buoyancy vests.

In developing markets venues may cut corners on safety, especially with temporary events that are gone the day after. Venue managers and event organisers possibly take a cavalier approach and hope that nobody will notice and the authorities will not bother because they will never see it. Or, organisers simply do not consider risks because they are not trained to think of them.

Safety practices, laws, enforcement and adherence vary from country to country. This is important to keep in mind not only for event organisers in developing markets, but for all event organisers who may engage a foreign client, or indeed a home client who places an event abroad.

In developed markets venues will be accustomed to adhering to health and safety regulations. Still, things do get overlooked.

An event organiser cannot assume that a venue is following safety regulations – especially with the temporary nature of events, set-builds and installations.

Because events tend to be one-off occasions, the normal working practices of venues and their staff get disrupted. People suddenly need to work in a different way, or at different hours, or do different things to their normal job. So, however familiar people are with their environment, the event organiser must view things as an outsider.

In unusual venues, or venues that would normally not host events, the event organiser must take care to 'walk in the footsteps of guests' during the planning and set-up stages. Are there any slippery floors, uneven surfaces, unlit steps or trip hazards? The flow of guests must be considered in unusual venues, too: are there enough exits, is there adequate signage, are there enough toilets?

Green-field sites present additional challenges to satisfying safety compliances, including the need for permits and permissions.

Events at green-field sites are usually large and require the attendance of a fire and/or safety officer and an ambulance crew.

Professional event personnel will be familiar with the FH&S regulations. The production manager will ensure all materials, drapes, scenery and sets are

A fashion show was held on the top level of a multi-storey car park with views of the city making a fine backdrop.

In usual circumstances, not everybody would arrive to a multi-storey car park at once. But, at a fashion event, the guests are provided with an arrival time.

So, the guest arrival times should have been staggered because the 500 guests could not fit into the two small lifts.

The queue of stylishly dressed guests snaked out of the door, along the street and around the corner.

Most guests gave up waiting for the lifts, so they decided to take the stairs. It was a ridiculous sight to see a spiral of guests in long dresses and high heels clambering up flights of back staircases – and car park stairwells are not the most glamorous places to expose to fashionable guests.

At the top level of the car park, everybody was arriving to the event with puffed cheeks and red faces.

This was a planning error by the event organiser which, although unprofessional, was more of an inconvenience for the invited guests.

However, the real problem could have been the emergency evacuation of 500 guests from the top level of a multi-storey car park with only two small lifts.

flame-retardant. If there is a car in the venue, the battery must be disconnected and the fuel tanks emptied of fuel and fuel vapour.

8.15.2 Safety legislation information

Fire Precautions Act 1971

Health and Safety at Work Act (HASAWA / HASWA)

Health and Safety Executive (www.hse.gov.uk)

Risk Assessment (www.hse.gov.uk/risk/)

Hazard Analysis (www.hse.gov.uk/risk/identify-the-hazards.htm)

Control of Substances Hazardous to Health (COSHH) Regulations 2002

Hazard Analysis and Critical Control Points (HACCP)

The Purple Guide to Health, Safety and Welfare at Music and Other Events (http://thepurpleguide.co.uk)

The Green Guide to Safety at Sports Grounds (http://greenguide.co.uk).

8.16 Aesthetics

All live events need to be aesthetic and most are required to be experiential for the guests to indulge their senses for optimum enjoyment of the experience.

Much planning would have gone into the look of the event, its layout and design, and the stage effect for the television and/or live audience.

These days, creative events get designed to excite all the senses: the look (colours, graphics, visuals, décor, pyrotechnics, special effects), feel (ambience, activities, giveaways), smell (food, flowers, perfume, aromas), taste (food, cocktails) and sounds (music, speeches, pyrotechnics, special effects, sound quality).

Consideration must be given to how televised or live-streamed events will look on camera. All angles and positions need to be considered. This includes lighting, staging, lecterns and backdrops. It also includes the cameras being able to capture logos on wide shots and tight shots.

It is necessary to ensure branding and promotional material is visible, particularly if there are sponsors who expect or have paid for exposure and association with the event, charity or cause. It is not good enough to have a drink sponsor's logo on the front of the bar, for instance, if it will be obscured when the bar is busy with people standing in front of it.

Branding may be subliminal or obvious, but must be visible.

The event organiser must plan where the celebrities will be photographed and erect a media wall covered with logos of the event and/or the sponsors. This will indicate to the celebrities where they should stand for photos, and it will gather the press in the place where the branding is located, rather than having them crowd the doorway or scatter throughout the venue where branded photo opportunities are wasted.

There are 'negative' aesthetics to consider, too.

Whatever the event organiser can see, the guest or member of the audience can see, also. But, this only works if the event organiser looks at the event from the audience's viewpoint.

If the coats are visible in the cloakroom, it must be screened; if there is rubbish behind a door that can be seen when the door is opened, the rubbish must be removed; if the bar staff have their coats piled in a corner behind the bar, the coats must be hung away.

8.17 The front door

An inexperienced event organiser might expect all the action to be inside the venue. In reality, the focus of action is at the front door.

There is a lot happening at the door: guest arrivals, VIP arrivals, drop-offs, people greeting each other, guest lists to scrutinise, passes to check, registration to process, security, press and paparazzi. Often, the cloakroom is shoehorned into this area, which adds to the commotion. With all this going on, just getting guests through the melee and into the venue can be an event in itself.

The front door is the first place to get busy and therefore becomes an instant priority for the event organiser. The danger for the inexperienced event organiser is in abandoning other areas because of the sudden attention that the front door demands.

But, if the demands of the front door are anticipated and planned, it is not sudden and will fit in with other areas that require attention. After all, it can be anticipated that the front door focus will happen at the start and end of the event.

To plan the front door, it is important to have an efficient and properly briefed door team who can check tickets or names against guest lists. Remember to order the guest list alphabetically, otherwise it is quite useless. They can fast-track VIPs and also control the press. With this efficiency in place, the event organiser can focus attention on the door – especially at the arrival and departure stages of the event – but can also float to other areas.

Often, the client will be at the door as a familiar face to receive and welcome guests. This is helpful in most cases, because the client will know whom to admit if somebody has misplaced or forgotten their invitation. Ensure the door team and the client are introduced, briefed and are working to assist each other. It all helps for smooth entry for the guests, which impacts their experience of the event.

Once the front door is running smoothly, the event organiser can check other areas in the general order of the flow of a guest moving through the venue: check the bar for speed and level of service; check the production box to ensure the production manager and crew are ready; check everything backstage is correct and ready. Then, back to the entrance to continue checking arrivals and the satisfaction of the client.

Once the flow of guests entering the event diminishes, the event organiser can turn away from this area.

Towards the end of the event, the event organiser will return to the front door to bid farewell to guests and receive their feedback.

Operational event management is a constant cycle of monitoring the event and checking everything . . . then, checking everything again.

Adopting this approach will arm the event organiser with an overview of the entire event. Every area will be visited, checked, observed and overseen. Intervention and guidance may be delivered to staff. By the end of the event, the event organiser will have a realistic understanding of what areas caused concern, if any, and will be in a position to effectively counter complaints, if any.

So, even from the very beginning of an event, the event organiser is preparing for the management procedures that will arrive post-event.

8.18 Cloakroom

After the front door has been negotiated, the guests find themselves at the cloakroom. The importance of the cloakroom is often overlooked and it can be viewed as an add-on to the event. This is especially so when a cloakroom is set up temporarily and is not already in situ at a venue.

Often, the cloakroom staff are under-trained and undervalued.

But, if there were no cloakroom at all, guests would be carrying coats over their shoulders, all evening.

The cloakroom is where guests enter the event and from where they depart. It is where they first and last encounter the quality of the service. Therefore, the cloakroom provides guests' first impressions of the event, and their last.

If a guest has to wait in a long queue to deposit their coat, it will interrupt their flow into the event at the time when they wish to get into the venue. If the same happens when collecting their coat, it will delay their departure at the time when they wish to get out of the venue. It will frustrate the guests, and if a coat is misplaced or lost, it is upsetting for them.

The event organiser should think about these effects and reflect on how it feels – or has felt – as a guest at an event.

A cloakroom must be correctly positioned and clearly marked. It should offer fast and friendly service. And, it must be secure – which means staffed at all times, not just at the beginning and end of the event.

Although guests may wish to deposit their coats as soon as they enter the venue, and will want to retrieve them as they depart, it does not always make sense to place the cloakroom just inside the entrance.

Consider the pressure on the front door, as discussed earlier. Placing the cloakroom in an already busy area may mean queues form outside the venue or the entrance becomes obstructed.

It *is* acceptable to place the cloakroom deep inside the venue, to draw guests out of the cold and rain, and away from the congestion of the entranceway, so long as the way to the cloakroom is clearly signposted.

It is worthwhile for an event organiser to listen to a weather forecast to ascertain the likely pressure on the cloakroom. At least, judge the season . . . and the country. It would be an error to feel that a cloakroom is not necessary for a midsummer event, when the weather forecast predicts showers.

It is important to screen the inside of the cloakroom from guests' view. Not only because it can look unsightly, but for security reasons. If a coat is misplaced, a guest can point to a beautiful designer coat and declare it as theirs. At the end of the event, one poor guest will go home with a not-so-wonderful replacement. This cannot occur if coats are not visible.

The need to train, brief and organise the cloakroom staff is often overlooked. But, the receiving, storing, securing, synchronising and retrieving of possessions that are valued by guests amount to a complex operation requiring organisational and interpersonal skills. It is a responsibility and the staff should receive adequate training to meet it.

Cloakrooms seem to be allotted the smallest corner of the venue and the staff often struggle to accommodate the coats. If this is the case, a mess can occur and coats will be misplaced or hung out of sequence. Some coats will have to be doubled-up on hangers, causing confusion, sequence problems and hidden tickets. It slows the entire procedure and guests have to wait too long, or a queue forms.

In small cloakrooms, coats will fall to the floor and become dusty or trampled. A guest will have to wait until the end of the event if the staff cannot retrieve their coat.

A cloakroom is not only for coats. Often, there is no provision for storing hats, umbrellas, laptops and tablets, bags and briefcases – even at post-conference parties and dinners.

In any of these situations, the frustrated and embarrassed staff will be on the receiving end of the wrath of the irritated guest. It would be unfair to place staff in such a position. The staff will judge their experience of the event as uncaring and disorganised, and that the event organiser was unprofessional. The guest will arrive at and depart from the event with the same conclusions.

Furthermore, the venue will look disorganised, which will affect its reputation. Unbeknown to the guest, it is neither the staff nor the venue that should be held to account. The event organiser is to blame for not *planning* the activity of taking coats.

It is helpful to place mirrors close to the cloakroom. It demonstrates attention to detail and is a courtesy. Ladies and gentlemen will wish to check their appearance when they dress.

But, mirrors should not be placed *at* the cloakroom, because it is already a congested area. Strategically placed, mirrors will encourage guests to dress away from the busy cloakroom.

It is always a nice touch to provide the door staff with large umbrellas to greet the arrival of limousines and taxis. Not only is it thoughtful and courteous, but if there are press in attendance, the front door provides a valuable opportunity for branded umbrellas to get photographed as VIPs arrive.

Chapter **9**

Inside the event

9.1 The guest experience

The restaurant industry measures the satisfaction of a diner by what is known as 'the meal experience'.

The model identifies everything the diner experiences from beginning to end. It is not only about the food on the plate.

So, the 'meal experience' actually incorporates much more than food. It includes the welcome, the standard of service, the level of lighting in the restaurant, the volume of background music, the entertainment, air conditioning, the cleanliness of the toilets and even the comfort of the chair. All this impacts the guest's *experience* of the *meal*.

An event organiser should adopt this approach by measuring the experience each guest will receive at the event: the *guest experience*.

Thinking this way, the event organiser must 'walk' through the event in their mind and consider the experience the guest will receive. It begins with the invitation, the marketing and the ease of getting to the venue. It includes the welcome at the front door, the queue at the cloakroom, the speed of service at the bar, the quality of catering, the entertainment, the sound and light, the efficiency of staff, the quality of the venue . . . right the way through to collecting their coat from the cloakroom, collecting a departing gift, being bid 'Goodnight' and exiting the venue. This is the model of the 'guest experience'.

So, the staff have been briefed and are in their places. The lights are in the correct mode and the background music is playing.

The final walk-round has been conducted and all areas of the venue are ready. The welcome staff are in place to receive tickets or invitations and count the number of guests entering the venue.

The waiters are pouring welcome drinks at tables inside the venue.

The doors are now ready to be opened.

This moment – the moment when the doors are opened for guests to enter the venue – is the culmination of the event organiser's job. All the meticulous planning, thinking of the detail, the safety considerations, negotiations with suppliers and the venue, the researching, sourcing and procuring, the meetings, discussions and site visits – all have been in preparation for this moment.

Now, it is only the *guest experience* that matters.

In effect, the guest experience begins with the guests' expectations . . . then, it is a case of having them met.

If the invitation is printed on good-quality card with gold edges, a guest's expectations will already be raised.

The principle can be equated with walking into a restaurant: expectations will be different for dining at The Ritz, or ordering at McDonalds.

This is not about comparing the quality of two restaurants, nor the guest's satisfaction with either experience. It is about *expectations*.

A hungry diner will be perfectly satisfied with McDonalds because the strict uniformity of each outlet ensures the diner's expectations are fully met. Whereas, expectations when dining at The Ritz may be so high that a guest could leave disappointed.

The planning of an event must anticipate guests' expectations. Then, they must be met.

At an event, there can be a range of guest categories, each of which needs satisfying. There is the client, the sponsor and the VIP guest. There may also be

AUTHOR'S VOICE BOX

Before Rihanna performed at the beach resort of Sopot in Poland, the event organisers cordoned off a large area of the beach solely for Rihanna to sunbathe.

Subsequently, members of the public were held back behind barriers where they gawped and photographed the megastar.

Rihanna was overhead complaining about being treated like an animal in a f***ing zoo.

It wasn't that Rihanna objected to being stared at – she flaunts herself in public all the time.

The problem was that the event organisers had their own interpretation of how a superstar would expect to be treated. In this case, they over-anticipated Rihanna's expectations and by doing so, they created a situation that made her feel awkward and unhappy.

seated guests and standing guests, balcony guests and stage-side guests, paying guests and non-paying guests . . . What are they each expecting? And, will those expectations be met?

With celebrities and VIPs, it is worthwhile for the event organiser to liaise with their agent, publicity manager or personal assistant to ascertain their likes, dislikes, requirements and dietary preferences. Such information will be stated on the entertainment rider if the celebrity/VIP is booked to perform or speak.

9.2 The press

Many event organisers decide not to like the press and paparazzi because they see them as being intrusive and aggressive. But the press have a job to do and many of them are freelance, which means that if they do not get the picture, they do not get paid.

An event organiser would do well to think how it would feel if the press did not turn up to the event.

Every event organiser wants the press to attend. And, they are desperate for the type of event that attracts press and media profile.

Press attendance is exciting – and is vital for the profile of the event and the venue. So, the press should be welcomed, just like all guests. But, they do need managing, just like all guests.

It is unprofessional to allow members of the press the freedom of the venue or provide backstage access without any restriction. Measures need to be in place to lead and guide the press, and control their behaviour.

Treated wisely, the press are the event organiser's dream, not their nightmare.

9.2.1 Press room

A private room with complimentary drinks and a buffet should be provided for exclusive use by members of the press. This is another reason for anticipating their numbers in advance.

AUTHOR'S VOICE BOX

At one awards event to recognise the notable achievements of women, the press were given freedom of the venue.

They crowded around the stage throughout the entire proceedings which obscured the view of the seated audience.

The event organiser did frequently try to wrangle them into a tidy situation, but every time another guest took to the stage to receive an award, the press repeated their pandemonium and jostled for position.

That lack of control made the event organiser appear unprofessional and the event look disorganised – which also reflected poorly on the venue because guests usually do not know or even think there is an event organiser.

At the same event, when it came time to enjoy a lavish post-awards buffet, the press were again given free access in the dining area. There they were, in their jeans and leather jackets, quaffing wine, filling their plates at the buffet table . . . and taking ad-hoc photographs of guests.

It was inappropriate for members of the press to be mixing with VIPs during food service. It meant the VIPs could not relax and enjoy the buffet. They needed to keep their guard up or they would be photographed with mouthfuls of food.

A press room has the advantage of keeping the press distant from the guests, allowing VIPs to relax without being hassled. It also helps the reporters and photographers to feel especially welcome, with press passes that provide access to their own private hospitality area.

The press room should provide information packs about the event. Brochures of the venue can be available for journalists to add details to their reporting. Contact details of the client or the PR representative should be available, too.

Be sure to supply good Wi-Fi and plenty of power points for laptops, iPads, cameras and smartphones.

If a press room is unachievable or unwarranted, the press should be given a time limit for photographs or interviews.

Otherwise, a *press-call* or *photo-call* should be arranged.

For photo-calls, it is imperative to have branding in place. Usually, this consists of a logo-branded backdrop, which is known as a *media wall* or *media flat*.

If press are not invited into the venue but must get their material outside the venue, or one media company is granted exclusive access whereas others are kept outside, a press pen should be created with barriers at a vantage point outside the front door of the venue. This will show the press where to congregate and keep them in a controlled environment.

Branding should be strategically placed at the entrance to be captured during interviews and photo opportunities.

For high-profile events with high press interest and celebrity attendance, it is advisable to create two lanes into the venue.

The 'normal' guests enter through one lane – the fast lane – whereas celebrities enter through another lane where they pause for photographs and interviews in front of the media wall.

This two-lane procedure allows for the free flow of 'normal' guests entering the venue, whilst providing them with the spectacle of seeing the celebrities and media commotion as they pass.

Not all venues have wide entrances that can accommodate the two-lane system, however. The Odeon in Leicester Square gets around the problem at royal film premieres by having normal guests arrive at an earlier time. When these guests are seated in the auditorium, a live camera at the front door relays the arrival of celebrities and is shown to the audience on the giant cinema screen. The royal patron is always scheduled to arrive after everybody else is seated. This last arrival is again broadcast on the screen for interest and to give added kudos to the occasion. It also helps the audience to stand at the correct moment.

The idea of a live camera at the front door for guests to watch celebrities arriving is not solely reserved for royalty – it is an idea that can be used at any event and any venue.

9.2.2 Press release

If the event is press-worthy, which may simply be down to celebrity or VIP attendance, a press release should be issued by the client or their marketing or PR representative. The event organiser will produce the press release if it is in their brief as part of the event management responsibilities. The purpose of a press release is to inform the media of the event and get them to request invitations or register for press passes in advance of the event. It is important to know how many press are expected at the event and which publications they represent.

Knowing which publications are represented helps the event organiser to anticipate the level of actual media interest and ascertain how many press to cater for and to control. It will also greatly assist afterwards with monitoring those publications for reports of the event.

9.3 Event photography

It is worthwhile to photograph every event for the portfolio and for future marketing purposes. It conveys experience of events, longevity in the industry, loyalty from clients and the diversity of events undertaken.

When pitching for events to first-time clients, a portfolio is essential for winning business.

A client needs to feel confident when awarding a project to an event organiser they have not used before.

Event proposals need to be creative. Images remain the most effective means of showing ideas: what they look like and how they work. Describing previous events does not always work – especially when speaking with a client who lacks creativity or imagination.

Even when the client or the venue has employed an event photographer for an event – a wedding will employ their own photographer, for example, or a conference client may video their conference – the event organiser should ask permission to bring their own photographer on-site.

This is because clients usually want photos of happy people, and a venue only wants shots that favourably show their facilities. But, an event organiser needs to build a gallery of setting up, branding, table layouts, theme and decoration, backstage scenes, team photos, food displays, cocktails, unusual creatives and VIPs. Shots such as these will convey professionalism and demonstrate versatility.

It is also helpful if the event organiser has an established relationship with the photographer so as to direct all those required shots, and not have to cajole the wedding snapper away from shots of the happy couple, to go into the kitchen to photograph the chefs.

The principle of having control applies just as much with a photographer as it does to security, music and all other elements that make an event a success – the event organiser needs to direct what they want and when they want it. This includes photos.

9.4 De-rig

The de-rig (from de-rigging) (or *break-down*) comes towards the end of the event when all the guests have left.

It is not uncommon to witness a de-rig beginning whilst guests are still in the venue – especially if they are the last few guests yet to depart. But, after all the meticulous detail and planning that went into ensuring guests received the best aesthetic experience, it is somehow damaging to permit any guests to see the stage being broken down or the chairs being unceremoniously stacked.

Pubs and nightclubs turn on the lights to encourage guests to get out. Events are not pubs or clubs.

It is unprofessional to expose the dirty work of a de-rig in view of guests. An event organiser would not invite guests to watch the set-up, so why show them the de-rig?

It is sometimes necessary to clear space whilst guests are in the venue – to allow room for dancing, perhaps – but this is considered a *turn-around*, not a de-rig: i.e. it is not the *end* of the event.

The turn-around can happen when dinner is cleared and tables are cleared from the dance-floor. Or, the guests can be encouraged into another room – the bar, for example – whilst the banquet tables are cleared and the room is cleared. This latter way is often the case at weddings.

The time it takes to de-rig must be calculated in advance because of the hire period of the venue. Penalties can be incurred for overrunning the hire period. Venues do allow an extended hire period for the de-rig, for which they may charge 50% of the daytime hire fee, and this is often negotiable.

At most events, the event organiser will be on-site to oversee the de-rig and ensure the venue is left in good condition.

At large events, however, the production manager will be wholly responsible for the de-rig and the de-rig crew, so the event organiser may not even be on-site after all the guests have left. Technical crews have their well-practised routines, so there is no reason for the event organiser to stay behind to get physically involved at this stage of the event.

9.5 Get-out

When everything is removed from the venue, the get-out is complete: this is the *get-out time*.

The get-out time will be the end of the venue hire period as stated in the venue contract. If the actual get-out is later, there can be hourly penalty charges.

Ideally, the planning would have allowed excess time for de-rigging the event so that the actual get-out time falls earlier than the contracted get-out time. The risk of incurring penalty charges should be minimal if the planning was done well.

An event is not over when the last guest has departed. The get-out time is the 'true' end of the event.

•   •   •

However, even though the get-out is complete and the event is truly over, there are still responsibilities that remain for the event organiser to execute.

These responsibilities are carried out in the post-event phase.

PART 4

Management post-event

.

Chapter **10**

Debriefs and reports

It can be tempting for an event organiser (and the client, too) to be lethargic about the responsibilities and procedures after an event.

After the lengthy lead-in during which all the research and planning were undertaken, and having then completed the event itself with the on-site logistics and execution, it is understandable to succumb to the anti-climax.

Furthermore, to settle any outstanding invoices for an event that has already passed into history is a bind.

On top of all this is the big problem of the next event. The next event becomes the first priority for an event organiser – especially a freelance who is under financial pressure to move on. Even in an agency business, there is pressure for the event organisers to get on with the next project and not enact the post-event procedures of their last event.

This can impact on not finishing the previous event properly – what is often referred to as the *mop-up*.

Post-event procedures are the aftercare.

It must be remembered that each procedure of event management forms the job as a whole. The procedures that occur post-event fit with the beginning-to-end management of an event: pre-event, on-site and post-event. This means that post-event management is one third of the whole. It cannot – must not – get ignored or be underestimated. One procedure missing will break the link.

Finishing the responsibilities determines the professionalism of the person.

An event will not be great without the pre-event procedures. Nor will it be great without the on-site procedures. So, there has to be an impact on the greatness of an event with the post-event procedures – however overwhelming is the urge to move on to the next project.

The answer to some would be that it does not matter! The event is over and was a great success. Move on.

If the event was not a great success, let's get over it, forget about it and make the next event better.

The question is: how can every event be improved on – successful or otherwise – if there is no post-event analysis, evaluation or learning?

This book is presented in three sections for a reason. This last third of events management will reveal the need and importance of the post-event procedures.

How an event organiser conducts the close of the event, post-event, is a continuation of the reflection of their professionalism. It also demonstrates their respect for those whom worked to ensure the event was successful – the client, the venue, the caterer and every contractor and service provider involved with the success of the finished event, just gone.

Here is the creation of the legacy.

Events is a specialised industry and this makes it an intimate business. People in events know each other and reputation is precious.

The previous event is the precursor to the next event. So, the finishing is as much about the next job as it is about the last job.

It is business. And everyone working in the events industry needs business.

10.1 Debriefs

Debrief meetings will be shown on the event schedule so that team members can expect the meeting, diarise it and keep to it as part of the project.

10.1.1 Management team debrief

Firstly, the event organiser should hold a debrief meeting with the event management team who worked the event.

This debrief happens before all others because it will provide the event organiser with information about the positives and negatives of the event before learning them from other parties.

The event organiser will thereafter be in a position to defend any issues and would have conducted an investigation, albeit a preliminary one, to understand what happened and what steps can be taken to placate the client.

This debrief occurs immediately after the event because the team have fresh reflections of the event and are likely to be available before moving on to other projects.

Often, the management team debrief will be scheduled for the day after the event.

This debrief is particularly helpful to identify learning points and what can be improved upon. It is an internal reflection and verification of performance.

10.1.2 Venue and suppliers debriefs

Supplier debrief meetings should be held with the major suppliers, such as the venue, caterer and production.

Once the event is over, the venue will wish to conclude any outstanding matters promptly – particularly outstanding payments. Probably, the only outstanding payments to the venue will be the unknown variable costs of food and beverage, which are dependent upon actual consumption at the event. Besides, the known fixed costs such as the venue hire fee and other required services that the venue is providing would have been paid during the planning phase, pre-event.

The venue debrief should occur after the management team debrief, otherwise there would be the temptation to debrief with the venue once the event is over – on the night. This would be logistically simpler. But, there needs to be a cooling period: time for reflection. If this is not allowed, the event organiser and the venue manager will merely have a chat and may not even be honest with each other. This would not be an objective meeting.

The problem, already, is that the event organiser can face a dilemma because the venue (and other suppliers) want immediate payment after the event has happened, but the event organiser has not yet confirmed the client's satisfaction with the event.

There are steps to deal with this which, if they are put in place before the event, will prevent conflicts arising after the event:

- Agree payment terms with the venue and any other suppliers that will be owed payments after the event. This manages their expectations and will provide valuable time for the event organiser to determine the satisfaction of the client.

- Conduct a short meeting with the client prior to the event but close to the date, so as to determine that all the finalised plans and decisions meet with their approval. This way, the client cannot surprise the event organiser after the event with complaints or unrealised expectations.

- Place a call to the client the day after the event to ascertain their satisfaction or any concerns they may have. This is a courtesy call and is not a debrief. It should come over as a 'thank you' call, but the underlying purpose is to determine the level of client satisfaction.

. . .

If these procedures are applied, the event organiser will have confidence to settle invoices promptly after the event.

Even if there is a complaint or a failure in meeting expectations, the venue and other suppliers should get paid as contracted and promised. Arguments can be worked out later. This way, any problems do not get exacerbated by the ill-feeling which arises due to late or withheld payments. If a complaint is justified and final payments have been settled, reimbursements can be made and claims can be submitted.

Event service suppliers work in the events industry. So, even if their service was unsatisfactory and the event organiser would not use them again, the supplier must be dealt with promptly and courteously. They will continue circulating with clients and competitors in the same industry, so the protection of one's own reputation is essential.

In any case, if the event organiser was performing the on-site management procedures well, he would already have highlighted good and negative aspects of the event, and would be aware of any issues that could be investigated after the event at the debriefs.

However, sometimes a supplier, such as a caterer, will inform the event organiser at the debrief of an issue that occurred during the event. It may be something akin to some guests complaining the food was too spicy, or the buffet had run out but was replenished within ten minutes. This information is important for the event organiser to realise before the client debrief occurs, because if the client raises these complaints, the event organiser can defend the complaint with prior knowledge and information.

Suppliers have depth and breadth of experience at events, and their evaluation after the event can be insightful and valuable.

So, an event organiser should wish to know whether the suppliers themselves had a positive experience at *this* event. Feedback from all sources is essential and is a measure of whether this job was done well. Again, it is for the protection of one's own reputation. An event organiser would not want suppliers reporting negatively to other suppliers and clients.

10.1.3 Sponsor debriefs

Where sponsors are contributing to the event, it is advisable for the event organiser to schedule debriefs with each sponsor, or the main sponsor.

Certainly, the client will be receiving feedback from sponsors, so the event organiser should meet with or place a phone call to sponsors so as to ascertain their level of satisfaction.

Were sponsors pleased with their exposure? Was their branding visible? Did their product get sampled? Was it well received?

Conducting a post-event phone call or meeting with sponsors is also a relationship-building exercise because the event organiser may wish to approach the sponsor for their generosity at a future event. To do so, however, relies on whether the sponsor's expectations were met, and on knowing how those expectations can be met next time.

10.1.4 Client debrief

Once the event organiser has received feedback from the management team, venue, other suppliers and sponsors, the client debrief can take place.

This debrief meeting will still be close to the date of the event – ideally, within the same week as the event.

By such time, the event organiser has gathered a good and reliable understanding of the merits and negatives of the event, and it should be unlikely that the client will raise an issue that is not already known about by the event organiser.

Conducting the other debriefs before the client debrief also allows time for the client to have received and analysed guest feedback (see 10.3), which can be discussed at the client debrief.

The client debrief is largely another relationship-building exercise. It is a courtesy to meet the client and ascertain the level of their satisfaction.

Where the event organiser is confident that the event was a success and the client is pleased, this debrief can be a social affair, such as a lunch or dinner, to thank the client, chat about the success of the event and discuss potential future business.

Meeting the client after the event does have its purposes in the procedures of event management, as outlined previously. Still, the event organiser's objective is to further develop the client relationship and secure another event.

Repeat business and client retention are all-important in the events industry where referrals and reputation win the jobs, and advertising one's services as an event organiser does not necessarily win new business.

• • •

Without the post-event debriefs, an event organiser does not learn whether they did a good job because the only other feedback is hearsay.

Even where the event organiser seeks feedback at the event – asking departing guests if they had an enjoyable evening, for example – it is mere courtesy and will most likely be met with a courteous response from guests. Especially where alcohol has been served, guests will reply with joviality. Such feedback cannot be treated as reflective, measured, structured and objective analysis.

If there are any issues held by staff, the venue, suppliers, sponsors or the client, the event organiser may not learn about them without debriefs.

It is easy for stakeholders to walk away after an event and not verbalise any disappointments or shortcomings – which are essential for the event organiser in order to learn and evolve their craft.

10.2 Complaint handling

If a client has a justified complaint, the event organiser should already be aware of the issue through their personal involvement during the event, or by learning about it from other parties during the post-event debriefs.

Just as with the planning phase, which eliminates any surprises occurring during the event itself, so the debriefs eliminate the chance of being surprised by a complaint.

Where a client does raise a complaint, the event organiser should be in a position to state this was already brought to their attention, and that they have arranged for the person or supplier who was responsible to learn from it. Thus, a situation can be defended and placated.

To be surprised is a management failure.

Prior knowledge of a complaint allows the event organiser to investigate the circumstances before the client debrief. It will also allow time for deciding what measures to take, such as a discount from the event management fee. This way, the client debrief meeting can be constructive and the client will feel satisfied and well-treated.

If the client feels they have a complaint, the event organiser must not avoid the subsequent phone calls or emails. Problems do not go away. Facing the client to discuss a problem really does work. Where a client has expressed dissatisfaction, the client debrief meeting provides the opportunity for both parties to discuss the situation.

So, the scheduled client debrief ensures a face-to-face meeting happens, whatever the outcome of the event. This is a good thing. Clients respond well to an event organiser who faces the problem, has investigated the situation and attends the client debrief meeting with a proposition.

It is not unknown for a client to invent a complaint so as to reduce the final bill. Again, if the event organiser has conducted on-site procedures and post-event debriefs, the legitimacy of the complaint will be known.

An event organiser cannot defend a position without full and reliable knowledge of what was positive or negative during the event.

Even if the complaint is unjustified and the event organiser recognises this is so, it does not preclude the offer of a compromise or goodwill gesture. It is still good client management. This should be seen as a learning opportunity. It may mean that the event organiser would not wish to work with this client again. Or, if they do, they will learn that next time it will require careful handling.

Where a supplier has failed and it has impacted the client's satisfaction, the event organiser must attempt to seek recompense, rather than simply blame the supplier. Remember, the client did not select the suppliers – this was the event organiser's job.

A client is contracting a specialist for their event and is paying for that specialist to appoint known and trusted suppliers.

It would be the event organiser who had made the wrong choice of supplier during the pre-event planning phase. This is why event organisers always use known suppliers with whom they have a trustworthy relationship.

An event organiser's suppliers are the event organiser's legacy.

10.3 Guest feedback

Although the client and the event organiser may each feel they have a fair idea of how an event went, it is not constructive to ascertain guest satisfaction solely on the basis of asking them if they had an enjoyable time as they leave the venue on the night of the event.

For one thing, guests will not wish to stay around to answer questions at any length, or enter into conversations about what was good and not so good about the event.

Anyway, from an *event management* point of view, guests are unlikely to know what should have gone better, what did not work, which objectives were not met, and many other aspects about an event that the event organiser and client had planned.

Realistically then, asking guests if they had a good time merely ascertains their level of enjoyment. This is just one measure of success. Besides, they may not answer honestly or their perspective may be skewed by alcohol. Asking, therefore, is a courtesy only.

Yet, guest feedback is as worthwhile as the debriefs, because other than asking those who sampled the experience of the event, there is no way for the event organiser to understand what needs to be improved.

If guest feedback is not gathered, the event organiser will not truly know what the visitors thought of the event, and there will be no measurement of whether this objective of the event was met.

Guest feedback, therefore, must be garnered in a constructive manner. This requires a procedural approach.

The event organiser may suggest to the client that they implement a short survey or questionnaire for guest feedback.

This can be achieved by email, or by the client selecting a sample of guests to contact for post-event feedback.

If attendees are company employees or conference delegates, an email questionnaire can be executed with speed and ease. Otherwise, the client should have an attendance list or guest database. If tickets were sold for a public event, a database will be required for the marketing and promotion of future events. This marketing database can be used for feedback purposes.

The guest feedback questionnaire need not be laborious or complex – the client will probably receive verbal feedback in the form of office banter, anyhow. But, it is important to ascertain levels of guest satisfaction or disappointments.

If the client is willing, the event organiser can introduce their own questions to the questionnaire so that feedback relates to aspects of event management pertinent to the event organiser's role, as well as the client's need to garner guest satisfaction.

A feedback questionnaire should reflect the objectives of the event. So, as well as ascertaining whether guests enjoyed themselves (which could be one of the objectives), there should be questions that provide feedback on other elements.

Some frequent feedback questions include: the quality of entertainment and the service; did guests find the venue easy to locate; was it easy to get there by public transport; was it easy to park close by; did guests like the choice of venue; was it clean; were the staff friendly; would they like the event to be held there again next year . . .?

Although guest feedback is gathered post-event, the preparation for this evaluation needs to happen pre-event in the planning phase. It will not work to start thinking after the event about how to gather guest feedback. If it is not planned, it will be too late, too slow to implement, another task to tack on, and by this time – after the event has happened – it will be difficult for the event organiser to get the client to bother with it.

Evaluation is part of the planning of an event, which is why the pre-event, on-site and post-event management procedures are interlinked to form the whole.

Pre-event, the event organiser should agree with the client what evaluation methods to use, which questions to ask, who will ask them, how big a sample of guests will be asked (or all guests) and when to action the questionnaire.

It is also important that guests are informed in advance that they will be approached for feedback. This way, they will be expecting the questionnaire when it arrives.

To motivate an optimum level of responses, a mechanism should be employed to encourage participants to complete and return their questionnaire. Such mechanisms can include a prize or a refund of their ticket price, or a free ticket to the next event.

Once feedback data has been received, it needs to be analysed and actioned. This enables the reflective evolvement of an event organiser's craft.

If appropriate, the data may be disseminated to other stakeholders.

10.4 Final report

After the client debriefing meeting has happened, the event organiser should compile a final report and insert it into the client file.

There is an example final report in Appendix VI.

This report is akin to a diary entry, with the event organiser's reflections and considerations.

The report makes note of points to remember, what worked well, what were the issues, what the client particularly liked or disliked, and any other thoughts that may assist the event organiser in the situation of the client asking to do the same event again.

Even if the client is unlikely to repeat the event, it may be that another client will ask for the same or a similar event or concept.

Because the final report becomes a useful and valuable document when an event reoccurs, even if it is not expected to reoccur, it must be completed for each event and all events.

One year later, or even three years after, when a similar event is commissioned, the final report will refresh the memory for the event organiser.

The final report is also useful as a reference for events taking place in venues that were used before. It helps avoid pitfalls and repeating mistakes.

The final report is the last documentation. It closes the file and symbolically ends the event.

• • •

Hopefully, the client will place another enquiry with the event organiser, even if it is for a different event or they have moved jobs themselves.

There are many clients, but for a client to find a trustworthy, knowledgeable event organiser who is fanatical about control, detail and eliminating risk, this need happen just once in their career.

The client relationship can be a strong bond. It is built on the foundation of trust.

As mentioned already, the guest experience is one barometer of success, and that happy guest just may be the next client or even another event organiser who is looking for evidence of loose cables, untidy bars and full bins behind kitchen doors that prove the worthiness or not of the organiser of the event. Do not ever let yourself down.

The success of an event is attributable to many components, many of which are described within this book. But, the success of an event is only guaranteed by the quality of the person organising it.

Happy Eventing!

Chapter **11**

Case studies

Client

The Crown Estate for HM Queen Elizabeth II

The brief

To produce a high-quality garden party in the grounds of the Royal Windsor Estate, to be attended by tenants of Her Majesty's property portfolio, the Crown Estate.

Other members of the Royal Household will be in attendance, including Their Royal Highnesses Princes Philip, Andrew and Edward.

• • •

The key element with this event was the green-field location in a royal garden that was open to public visitors. The build, the event itself and the de-rig needed to have zero impact to public visitors and to the flora in the garden.

Preparation and build needed to happen around the opening times of the garden and not restrict visitor access, many of whom were paid members.

Strictly no plants or flowers were to be damaged during the event, which included the lush green grass. No vehicles were permitted on the lawns.

This event required erecting a marquee to accommodate a tea party for 500 guests. It was decided to erect a soft-wall structure with see-through front panels that could be rolled down if it rained during the event. The interior of the marquee would be lined and there would be crystal chandeliers, levelled hardwood flooring, carpeting and good-quality tables and chairs. An additional side marquee would facilitate the kitchen.

Temporary trackway was laid to protect the lawns from service vehicles. The build would happen as near to the event date as possible, and the de-rig would begin as soon as the event had ended so as to prevent the grass from yellowing due to light starvation.

Temporary power and water were required for the lighting, kitchen equipment and tea urns.

High-quality mobile toilet facilities were hired.

The English weather being a factor, the red carpet walkway across the grass and into the marquee would be laid on trackway and absorbent coconut matting.

Management logistics

- Delivery, build, dismantling and removal of marquees
- Delivery, installation and removal of furniture
- Installation and removal of toilet facilities, power and water
- Delivery and installation of kitchen equipment, power and water
- Delivery and storage of catering
- Service of tea and cakes to 500 guests
- Budget management
- The Queen and Princes would be in attendance for one hour
- Royal protection service personnel would be in attendance.

Event debrief notes

It *did* rain on the morning of the event, which meant constant cleaning of the red carpet. Fortunately, the rain had stopped by the time the royal entourage arrived.

Guests arrived and were served tea and cakes before the arrival of The Queen.

Local schoolchildren were invited to line the grass route to the marquee. They waved flags and cheered as each member of the royal family passed through.

Among the smart-suited guests, it only became apparent which were members of the royal protection team by the way they stood to attention as the national anthem was played.

After the event had taken place, the only evidence was a small patch of dead grass where a waiter had emptied a hot water urn. He was reprimanded for this.

CASE STUDY 2 by Philip Berners: Artist and VIP hospitality at The BRIT Awards

Client

The BRIT Awards

The brief

To design, construct and staff the restaurant, bar, lounge area and entertainment facilities for all performers, presenters, hosts and VIP guests attending The BRIT Awards.

• • •

The BRIT Awards is the largest British music industry event with a live audience in excess of 2,000 and a television audience of over 6 million.

The design of the backstage hospitality areas needed to be innovative and sensational, as befitting an international music event with iconic music stars such as Cher, David Bowie, Whitney Houston, Sting, Bono, Robbie Williams, Tom Jones, Annie Lennox, Eminem and Stevie Wonder.

The backstage hospitality facilities were allocated a one-day build. The facilities needed to be operational for two rehearsal days and the event day itself. The de-rig must occur the day after the event. This made it a five-day operational event.

The restaurant menu had to be quick, easy, filling and excellent quality. Fruit and vegetarian dishes had to be prominent.

Management logistics

- Design of the restaurant, bar, lounge and entertainment areas

- Installation and build of the bar, lounge and entertainment facilities

- Daily food and beverage deliveries

- Stock security and management

- Staffing the bar and restaurant between 10 am and 11 pm on the two rehearsal days

- Staffing the bar and restaurant between 10 am and midnight on the show day

- Service of food and drink

- Maintaining quality of presentation of food

- Maintaining the standards of presentation in the backstage VIP areas.

Event debrief notes

A massive event with over 30 divisional managers and producers, this was a fun event in which to participate, but the logistics were demanding. The need to have constant deliveries of fresh food, plus to communicate backstage and front of house, meant the event team had possession of coveted Access All Areas passes.

The two rehearsal days were long and slow because each artist arrived for their one-hour rehearsal slot. The first rehearsal began early and the last finished late. The services needed to be available until the last rehearsal had completed. Mostly, the artists did not require a meal because they arrived from their hotel, did their rehearsal, then left the site. Mainly, their entourage came in for tea or coffee whilst the artist rehearsed.

The event day began early and was hectic all the way through the morning arrivals of performers, the afternoon dress rehearsal, the evening event and the post-event party. Then came the overnight de-rig.

CASE STUDY 3   by Philip Berners: Worldwide launch of the Bon Jovi album, *Crush*

Client

Universal Music

The brief

To source a destination that would be accessible for guests and press attending from Europe and Asia for the launch.

The launch activities comprised a private dinner for the band and record executives, a press conference, one-to-one press interviews, a celebrity launch party for 500 VIP guests, and a screening of the film *U-571* featuring Jon Bon Jovi.

Accommodation was required over three tiers: for band and record label executives, for invited guests and for journalists.

•   •   •

Although the brief was received six months prior to the event date, the first priority with this event was the location. We visited the *Confex* international event and destination exhibition for ideas and chose three concepts for the client to consider. The first was to stage the event in an ancient medina in Morocco. The second concept was to hold the launch aboard a cruise ship, with guests embarking at one destination and disembarking at another. The third was to launch the album on a floating barge in Venice.

All three proposals were ruled out because they had been done before. So, we settled on Italy as the destination and travelled to Sorrento, Ravello and Positano on the Amalfi coast, then to Naples and Rome to scout for venues.

Because of the logistics of the range of activities surrounding the event, and the three-tiered accommodation requirements, it was decided that Rome offered the most suitable location.

A five-star hotel on the outskirts of central Rome was selected as the lead hotel for the band, record label executives and event management team. Three hotels were chosen for the 500 invited guests. Another separate hotel would accommodate international journalists.

Band security was supplied by the record label. However, hotel security was sourced by the event team.

The press conference would be held in the 'Winter Garden' at the lead hotel, followed by a photo-call at the swimming pool.

There would be two days of one-to-one interviews with band members. These would be conducted in specially adapted suites at the hotel.

In the early evening, Jon Bon Jovi was to be filmed with a fan who had won a competition to have lunch with him. The event team were to act as other diners in the restaurant. Following this, there would be a presentation of a commemorative disc to mark the band's 100 million sales.

In the late evening, a candlelight supper was to be served to the band and record label executives in the lush botanical gardens of the lead hotel. Whilst this was happening, invited guests would be transported to a privately hired cinema to watch the screening of U-571.

After the executives' supper and the film screening, the band, record label executives, invited guests and journalists would converge at the lead hotel to attend the themed launch party.

The concept of the party followed a 'Crush' theme (the album title), with cocktails served over crushed ice and a 12-ft bar carved entirely from ice and frosted with the title of the album. Roman god torsos were carved from ice and used as vodka luges.

The Cinecittà film studios outside Rome were visited to source props to theme the party and it was hoped to have the ice carved locally. But, it proved more reliable to use trusted suppliers, so all elements were transported by road from London.

Two ice-carvers were flown from London to Rome, so as to place the bar, make last-minute adjustments and dismantle the ice afterwards.

Management logistics

- The band would be on-site for three days
- Accommodation arrangements for band, record executives, 500 guests and press
- Accommodation arrangements for event team
- Transfers from airport to hotels
- Transfers from hotels to screening; then screening to party; then return to hotels
- Sourcing of notable local restaurants for band
- Hire of screening venue
- Hire of party venue
- Hire of limousines for band and entourage
- Standby car
- Security
- Tiered security passes
- Party guest list management
- Branding for press conference
- Technical arrangements for press conference
- Photo-call
- Interview suites
- Executives' supper
- Decoration style for party, decoration team, transportation from London
- Food and beverage requirements
- Budget management.

Event debrief notes

The success of this event was in the planning. The pre-sourced arrangements, such as security, transportation, accommodation, hotel liaison, restaurants and menus, were crucial because our offices were in London. We conducted three pre-event recces and were on-site three days before the client arrived for the event. We departed Rome two days after the event.

Donatella Versace attended the party with seven bodyguards and a huge bouquet of red roses for Jon Bon Jovi.

The ice bar was a success and was widely featured in the press. Italy's glitterati attended the party and that generated much press also.

CASE STUDY 4   by Chantal Dickson: The 2014 Tour de France Grand Départ, Leeds

July 2014 saw the UK, in particular the Yorkshire region, hosting the first three stages of the Tour de France.

The cycling event consisted of three race stages commencing in Leeds and spanning 515 km. There were 144 riders in the men's race and 98 riders in the women's race. An estimated 2.3 million spectators lined the route of which 1.1 million were non-local residents. 177 global territories broadcast the race, viewed by more than 6 million people around the world.

The event was managed by six key stakeholders:

- ASO (Amaury Sports Organisation) – a commercial body, owners of the Tour de France.

- Welcome to Yorkshire – the main contract holder for Stages 1 and 2, and for Stage 3 outside London.

- Leeds City Council – the lead local authority.

- Local authorities – event organisers within their own authority boundaries.

- Transport for London – the contract holder for Stage 3 within London.

- UK Sport – Government sports agency providing the route with £10m funding, assurance of the programme, and expertise in major events.

Dubbed 'the people's tour', the coalition of stakeholders set the main aim for the event as '. . . to stage a sporting spectacle that would showcase our country across the rest of the world' and set four key objectives to help achieve this:

1   Enhance the reputation of Yorkshire to deliver world-class events.

2   Secure significant economic benefit for the region and the wider UK.

3   Inspire a legacy of cycling and increase participation in the sport.

4   Showcase the creativity and enthusiasm of the local Yorkshire communities.

The event faced two main challenges:

1   Local residents did not understand what the event was.

2   Local residents did not understand what the event included.

The coalition of stakeholders created and developed a comprehensive community engagement strategy based around encouraging communities to work together. At the centre of this strategy was a ten-day cultural programme designed to showcase and celebrate the Yorkshire region by showcasing the region's finest creative talents on a national and international stage. This festival ran for the 100 days leading up to the Grand Départ. This was also the first cultural festival to be held alongside the Tour.

The second element was for Welcome to Yorkshire to create the Tour Maker volunteer programme in conjunction with Asda. A total of 8,000 people were recruited and trained in a variety of roles from welcoming international visitors, to supporting the emergency services and being a friendly and reassuring face at the event. Embracing the ethos of 'happy to help' (which was printed on their uniforms), the programme was deemed a success with the volunteers being central to creating a celebratory atmosphere for all involved.

In addition to these core strategies, the key stakeholders also considered the legacy of hosting the event by creating the Tour de Yorkshire, an annual cycling race in the professional cycling calendar consisting of 8,000 amateur riders and sponsored by Maserati. Furthermore, in Leeds, the host of the ceremonial launch of the Tour called the Grand Départ, the Cycle Superhighway between Bradford and Leeds was built to encourage residents to continue to engage with cycling longer term. The Tour de France was worth an estimated £102 million to the Yorkshire region.

CASE STUDY 5   by Paul Glover: A circus celebration event in London

My company was asked to deliver an opulent extravaganza at a central London location by a famous circus family who had been delighting international audiences for 100 years.

The budget was generous at £500,000 because circus people love a spectacle – after all, spectacles are their business.

For this budget they expected absolute perfection for the guests which included royals, Hollywood actors, celebrities and political figures. So, I had to get it right: the reputation of my company depended on it.

Like many events of this magnitude the first issues arose over location and date. I had just six months' 'build out' which, in event terms, can be gone in a blink.

My first thought was to erect a Big Top marquee in either Regents Park or Hyde Park. But, both spaces were booked three years ahead. As the clock ticked down, I was delighted to find a West End theatre just off Leicester Square that seemed the perfect venue for such a grand occasion.

On the venue walk-round, my client loved the intimate feel and Victorian splendour of the historic theatre. For me, there was a bonus: the theatre had a well-fitted commercial kitchen from which my chefs could work. This meant there was no need to bring food on-site from elsewhere. Happy clients, happy me. Until the client threw the inevitable curveball . . .

'This all looks fine,' my client enthused, 'but, where will you put the animals?'

This was a pivotal moment in client relations, the kind that can make or break a deal. There is always something that a client forgets to say at the brief, or that they have thought about after negotiations have been finalised. This behaviour is hardly ever intentional but it nearly always happens.

Suddenly, I was standing on the shifting sands of client expectation. 'What animals?' I choked out.

'You know,' my client said, as if I *should* know, 'our four Indian elephants.'

It transpired that the circus owner wanted his pets at the celebrations!

Managing situations like this is what makes great event organisers stand out from the rest. The secret is not to be surprised, but to expect the inevitable and have a well-defined crisis management methodology to deal with such situations. There are few industries in which crisis management is an everyday occurrence, but event organising is one.

I managed to convince the theatre manager to let me bring the beasts along and the event was a huge success. In fact, four fully grown Indian elephants parading through an old London theatre created press headlines all over the world, and the BBC decided to produce a three-part special on the life of circus families.

After the event, I was left with just one problem at the de-rig: who was going to shovel 300 kilos of elephant dung?

CASE STUDY 6 by Ariane Lengyel: Grand party at the Palace of Versailles

When organising an event, it is often said and repeated that every last detail has to be checked, and checked again, so that the event goes smoothly. This case study is an example of how to expect the unexpected.

Just a few years ago in Paris, a large American company organised an incentive trip for its staff and partners. There were over 1,000 participants spread over several Parisian hotels. The trip was being organised on a grand scale. The participants were taken to visit the sites of the City of Light and entertained at the famous Moulin Rouge. The gala evening was the special event of the trip. The Hall of Mirrors at the Palace of Versailles was the venue chosen for the event.

Some history: the Palace of Versailles became a royal palace in 1661. The palace is famous for being the home of the French King Louis XVI and his wife Marie-Antoinette. It is a magnificent palace, decorated in the most ornate fashion, dripping in gold leaf and plush furniture. The Hall of Mirrors is the most well-known room in the palace and a very unique venue for a gala dinner. The organisers certainly had located one of the most exclusive venues in the world.

In order to make the event even more exceptional, period costumes were arranged for all the guests with the men in Louis XVI costume and the women in Marie-Antoinette dresses. The dresses that were worn by the women at that time were very wide and rested on a metal frame that was worn under the dress to keep the shape.

As the guests started arriving to get on the coaches to take them from the hotel to the palace, the organisers realised there was a big problem. Because of the size of the dresses, the ladies were unable to sit down on the coach as they could not fit into the seats. The dilemma was how to get the guests to the venue. The organisers had to think quickly and hired several more coaches so that the ladies could stand in the aisles for the 12-mile journey to the palace from central Paris.

This example shows how important it is to check every last detail when you are organising an event. The organisers probably did not think to get on a coach wearing a Marie-Antoinette costume . . . but they should have.

CASE STUDY 7   by Amira Malek: Reflections on graduating with an events management degree

When I thought of working in events, I dreamed of helping people experience amazing weddings and parties. However, the reality is that I am working in a completely different sector of the event industry and I am enjoying every aspect of it.

The events industry is vast, from creative entertainment events to corporate events, and encompasses a variety of roles such as set design, catering, logistics, technical support and overall management. It is a very demanding yet rewarding career to follow. I often work long hours and weekends, engage with multiple suppliers and meet deadlines simultaneously. This is all balanced by the overwhelming feeling of success when an event comes together and I have a pleased client and guests. It is a high-pressure, fast-paced industry so dedication is key.

Studying events management prepared me with the necessary skills for a job in this industry. While the course gave me some practical experience, it was not sufficient to prepare me for the intensity of working in the field. However, from a logistical perspective the events degree really helped me formulate an idea of what to expect, and taught me lots of useful skills, especially accounting, planning and industry practices.

I now work for a creative events production company that specialises in technology and videogame-based events. We organise launches of new games and products as well as showcasing them at expositions and shows around the world. Our goal is to present the game or product in the best way possible while providing an amazing experience for the fans or press who are our guests.

Working with worldwide clients has its limitations and sometimes we have to scale back our creative side to fit within brand guidelines. Managing clients' expectations is an acquired skill.

Whether it is weddings or gaming, the key factors of event management remain the same, which are the budget the client has to spend and their vision of how the event will be.

It is this balance which makes the difference between a profitable, reputable event business and one that is not. Managing the client's expectations within their budget parameters is a challenge the company and its staff face on a daily basis.

CASE STUDY 8   by Dr Evangelia Marinakou: An international IT conference in Greece

This case study discusses the low participation and engagement of attendees at an international conference and how the organisers could have engaged them more with the use of social media.

The FEMIS research conference is held every December in Rhodes, Greece. On average 200 people from finance, economics, management and IT attend the conference each year, mainly academics who are interested in presenting their research. The duration of the conference is only two days with a welcome cocktail event in the afternoon of the first day, and the presentations taking place on the second day. An informal dinner at the end of the second day is offered only to those close to the organiser from the university.

As the hotel event manager, I was asked to plan and organise the conference in our hotel. A meeting took place with the organiser from the university who was presented with different ideas on planning the conference, as well as how to improve and increase participation with the use of social media. In addition, different audio-visual equipment was presented at an extra cost in addition to renting the meeting room (which included coffee breaks); however, the organiser was not willing to cover this extra cost to add value to the presentations.

The whole event was held in a meeting room in the hotel and offered the possibility for participants to present their paper via overhead projectors with transparencies, which is considered to be an outdated method for presentations. I paid close attention to the event in order to observe the use of the overhead projectors as well as the participants' attendance to the whole event and other activities such as lunch.

To my surprise, most of the attendees did not use the projector and they were very frustrated that there was no digital projector. In addition, most of the attendees came to the event, gave their presentation and left right after, leaving a few having lunch and taking photos and even fewer staying until the end, which was a Friday afternoon. Later in the afternoon on the second day, many attendees were discussing the low attendance and they were surprised that most people had left before or after lunch. Finally, only five people accepted the invitation to have dinner with the organiser.

It was evident that the lack of proper IT and negligible use of social media to enhance the participants' engagement contributed to the limited participation at the event. Lunch was paid for by 50 people, yet only 27 attended. After a discussion with the organiser, I was informed that all photos were sent at a later stage via email. Moreover, the organiser neither provided the attendees with a list of the participants' details nor allowed for any further communication with, for example, a social media group that would have enhanced communication and engagement amongst the participants.

CASE STUDY 9 by David Titley: Reflections on studying for a degree in events management

During my first year at the University College Birmingham (UCB), aged 18, I worked part time at Twickenham Rugby Stadium in West London as a supervisor of corporate hospitality events. After I had completed my first year at university, I managed to secure a placement year at Twickenham. It was unusual for a student to enter into a placement after just one year of studying; however, with my previous experience at Twickenham, I felt capable of doing the opportunity justice.

I later realised that doing my placement after my first year was very beneficial to the remaining two years of my degree.

On placement, I made a conscious effort to work in as many departments of the venue as possible so that I could get a real idea of what it takes to run a large conferencing and events centre. In my 12 months at Twickenham, I had experience as a chef, cellar porter, kitchen porter, event set-up supervisor, bar supervisor, retail bar manager, retail bar IC (in control), human resources and recruitment assistant, events co-ordinator/planner, events supervisor and eventually an events manager.

After working full time at Twickenham for a year, I felt ready to take on the world, with or without the degree.

I questioned whether going back to university was the best thing to do with the wealth of experience that I had gained. So, I left UCB and continued living and working in London, moving from venue to venue to get as much part-time work as possible.

After speaking to my manager at Twickenham, I realised that I had been hasty, and not fully taken advantage of the experience I had gained. But he told me that I had gained something which most events management students my age do not have: genuine and productive event experience in a professional venue.

It was then that I realised I still had a lot to learn, and the best place to do that for me was at university. So, I managed to secure an unconditional offer at the University of West London (UWL).

Whilst studying at UWL, I continued to work in hospitality events in sports and leisure venues around the country, including Twickenham. Whilst studying, I felt my experience in events was complementing my degree more than my degree was helping my job.

Most of the theory-based assessments I received had to be related to 'experience in events', and the experience that I had gained was very relatable. One prime example was in the Event Design module in my second year where I was tasked to think about an event that I had been to or worked on, and talk about how the event design helped create a journey for the customer and immersed them into the event. I instantly thought about an event I worked on at Twickenham for The Royal Bank of Scotland (RBS) who were sponsors of the Six Nations Championship. RBS held an event in one of our function rooms, and the event theme was a rugby changing room. The event set-up team spent an entire week transforming the function room into a rugby changing room, that was also practical to serve food and drink to 500 guests.

In my assignment, I was able to write about how the event was designed from start to finish in great detail. This particular assignment did, in a sense, teach me what I already knew, but without knowing it. I had only viewed the RBS event design from my work perspective, and the module taught me how to see it from a guest's perspective; how to step back and create and analyse an atmosphere that immerses all senses to create an exciting journey for the guests.

As much as the Event Design module and my work experience complemented each other, without my experience of working in events, I would not have gained a thorough understanding of the assignment and received such a high grade.

This brings me onto a popular debate topic in events management teaching: practical teaching versus theoretical learning.

When the topic of practical vs theory comes up, I cannot help but think of a time at work when I had 500 guests arriving in half an hour; my temporary bar unit had stopped working and was leaking beer everywhere; I had only half of my allocated staff members; and my client was shouting in my ear and worrying if we were going to be ready on time. All these problems arose from external factors out of my control, yet I was the one responsible for fixing them.

When I reflect upon my degree, I try to think of a time when I was taught or given experience of how to think on my feet and stay calm in stressful situations. The reality is, there was no such teaching. The truth is that a student in a classroom cannot be taught experience. I do understand that to teach someone how to meticulously plan an event in great detail will lessen the chance of things going wrong. However, anybody who works in events will know that things can always go wrong to some degree. In my experience, dealing with these situations efficiently and professionally is a vital part of being a successful event organiser.

The question I am drawn to ask is, how do you teach this at university? My degree course provided the opportunity to plan and execute an event through the Live Event Management module, but the one live event I was tasked to organise was on a very small scale and was not a realistic challenge.

Every student had to complete a mandatory 400 hours of events experience for another module, but this may not necessarily provide the student with relevant experience.

I do feel that if a university is serious about preparing students for the real world of organising events, and making their graduates the best possible event organisers they can be, each student should need to work a full-time placement in a relevant events job for at least six months before graduating. Not only would this make them more prepared for working in events, it would also put them in a better position for employment and they would be able to relate the classroom teaching with real event experiences.

I think the practical side to teaching events management is as important as the theory. I believe teaching the theory of events will put the student in the right frame of mind to work in events, and they will probably achieve a higher classification of degree. However, I believe the practical elements of teaching will make a stronger events organiser.

The question I pose for academics is, what will event employers want when they recruit a graduate from an events course? Will they want someone who is capable of passing an exam and writing an essay, or will they want someone with knowledge of events and practical experience in planning and executing them?

The theory elements of my degree were important for my job as President of the Student Union. The Managing People module has given me confidence with running my team of 40 and I have an understanding of my responsibilities as an employer, both legally and ethically. The Finance module also helped with my job as I am responsible for the Student Union finances.

I think one of the best advantages of a degree in events management is the varied modules that are applicable to many industries. The degree develops many transferrable skills for use in any other industry.

Chapter **12**

Event management
as a career choice

A career in event management is quite often not a choice. In both developed and developing markets many organisers of events find themselves doing the role through necessity or by accident.

It may be a professional conference that needs organising, or a social party for Christmas to be planned. Once it is done, the organiser often finds they are asked to do it again next time round. If the organiser is good at doing it – and enjoys it, even – organising events becomes their job.

The good news is that anybody can become an event organiser: just like anybody can become a hotelier or restaurateur. Even parents find themselves organising the wedding of their offspring.

This provides an open doorway for anybody to walk through. But, it is also the main problem with the industry. Nobody needs a licence to organise an event. Qualifications and study are not required. Consequently, there are good event managers and not so good ones: just like there are good and not so good hoteliers and restaurateurs.

For those who *do* choose event management as a career, universities offer tailored courses. But, out there in the industry proper, events are still largely organised by people who found their way into event management by accident or default. In developing countries, there is no opportunity to study event management, anyhow.

The analogy with hotels and restaurants is appropriate because the hospitality (or *service*) industry is closely associated with events.

There tends to be crossover between a job in a hotel or restaurant and a career in events. In fact, working in a hotel provides the best starting point for the events enthusiast as they will gain experience in guest service, quality and standards, food and beverage, and conferences and banqueting.

With events – just as it is in hotels and restaurants – reputation is so important. Credibility is the control mechanism for the event industry. It is the credibility of each event organiser which upholds the industry's professional standards and informal benchmarking. It is what wins and loses clients.

That is why it is vital to be considered a good event organiser.

To become a 'good' event organiser is achieved by training or experience. Ideally, it would be a blend of the two. University courses in event management offer much theoretical knowledge, but courses often struggle to provide practical training. Thus, it is experience of organising events which determines how good an event organiser becomes.

If qualifications are not the necessary asset, then it must be experience. It would not be going too far to suggest experience is more sought after in the events industry than qualifications.

A qualification in event management allows the graduate to apply for management positions. It means that person knows *how* to do the job. Experience demonstrates they *can* do it.

Employers want both. Clients want the latter.

To gain experience in event management, it would make sense to select a position in a closely related industry. Jobs in marketing and PR are obvious examples that would bring one into close contact with events.

But, events are not limited to marketing and PR. Entertainment companies, record labels, fashion brands, even pharmaceutical companies . . . they all produce events. Most companies have a need for conferences, client hospitality receptions or an office Christmas party.

It does not even need to be a job in the events division of a company that leads to a career in event management. It does not matter whether one is working the bar or cleaning the floor – opportunities present themselves. Transfers between departments are an opportunity. Meeting people and networking is another.

Venues are possibly the easiest, quickest and most certain way to gain experience of events. There are many and various venues, so opportunities exist everywhere. It need not be a dedicated venue, such as a conference centre, sports stadium or concert venue, because unusual places host events, too. Galleries, museums, libraries, country houses, theatres, nightclubs ... wherever there is a live happening, there is a live opportunity to work at an event.

Other than venues, hotels still offer the best starting place for a career in event management.

Hotels offer a learning environment that is valuable and varied, and provide transferable skills that fit well with event management.

Again, it is not necessary to work in the conference and banqueting department of a hotel. The attention to detail, quality standards, guest service skills, organisational skills, leadership skills, teamwork skills and knowledge gained in the food and beverage departments are all prerequisites of a good event organiser.

Hotels host events, of course. If your interest lies with events, it will not take very long before a job in a hotel – whatever job that may be – brings you into contact with a conference, awards ceremony or a party.

There are many reasons why people become event managers. As mentioned, it can occur by chance or accident.

Also, it is a job that is perceived to offer variety, excitement, creativity and glamour, and that is why people choose it.

With events moving out of hotels and into unusual venues, they are more exposed to the public. This is another reason people choose to work in the events industry.

Televised events such as fashion shows, awards ceremonies, festivals and concerts also provide exposure of the industry to would-be organisers.

And, many young people who are looking for a career choice attend concerts, festivals and weddings, and decide they would like to be involved with organising them.

At the upper levels of event management, there are big budgets, world-renowned venues, travel and the opportunity to meet pop stars, celebrities and all manner of famous people. It is not surprising that people are attracted to a career as an event organiser. It is a bit like wanting to be an airline steward or to work on a cruise ship.

The guests on a cruise do not get to see the grime of the engine room. Airline passengers do not see the considerable preparation that happens before they board the plane. And guests at events do not see what goes on behind the scenes. Neither should they.

For an event organiser, the most exciting aspect of managing events *is* what happens behind the scenes: the backstage preparations, the control room or the production office. The enjoyment is in seeing what others do not get to see.

When people insist that it must be amazing to produce events for celebrities, they do not stop to understand it is work. The event organiser is there to do a job, not socialise with VIPs and fawn over celebrities. It is important to do the job well. An event organiser will not get the next job, otherwise.

Instead of kicking back with rock gods and Hollywood actresses, the good event organiser is thinking about timings, lighting levels, the music, and whether the canapés are hot enough.

So, the best thing about organising events for famous people is not being there with them, but being able to talk about it afterwards.

Although the engine room of events is out of sight and grimy, organising events for a living can reap plentiful rewards. Independent event organisers have unlimited earning potential. If they are good at their job, professional and experienced, they will retain their client base and then there are no limits . . . except for that matter of reputation.

In-house event organisers within organisations get to do the same job as a freelance, but without worrying about from where the next client is coming. Theirs is a regular salary and a touch more stability and security. Being within a company means that an in-house event organiser becomes the client. This is rewarding in itself.

I have been on both sides of the fence: I have worked as an independent event organiser and also as an in-house event organiser for corporations. The former requires the additional and vital input of sales . . . and being adept at maintaining client relationships. It is a competitive industry and clients are not always loyal. Even when clients are loyal, they are free to change their event organiser and try somebody new, who may have fresh ideas.

The latter – working as an in-house event planner for an organisation – can be claustrophobic, especially if the events are routine. The problem can be that event organisers are creative by nature, whereas chief executives, senior financial officers and shareholders are animals that instinctively follow the urges of revenues and expenditure. Creativity can suffer in environments where expenditure must be minimal and profit is required to be optimal. For a passionate event organiser, creativity is essential.

The most exciting aspect of organising events is the diversity. It is true that some people specialise in one genre of events – wedding planning or business conferences, for example. Or an event organiser may be employed in a venue that is limited in its range of events by the four walls. These limitations aside, event organisers can be as creative as they wish.

There are few drawbacks to being the event organiser within a good corporation, or within an exciting venue, or freelancing with excellent clients and high-profile charities.

Even venues that host events as secondary to their core business (museums, galleries, nightclubs or theme parks, for example) will realise the value of additional revenue from events, so there is room for the event organiser to shine brightly.

When the London Hippodrome broke onto the corporate events circuit, their events business increased from just four per year to over 100. This provided a significant contribution to the core business.

The contribution of revenue from events to the core business at Thorpe Park increased to a level where the organisation culture shifted. Opportunities were created to further expand the events offering and so the events department grew to become the only revenue-generating department during the closed winter season.

Where a national economy is experiencing a downturn, recruitment is often suspended and marketing gets cut back. Budgets are reduced, of course. It is commonly perceived that events suffer, too. Companies must be seen to reduce their expenditure and it does not bode well for an organisation to be partying in Cannes when jobs are being shed.

Experience shows that corporations *do* spend just as much on events during economic crises, but they do not shout as loudly about it. A corporation may not send 300 of its sales representatives to attend a conference in Cannes, but they will send thirty executives instead. And the budget will be just the same. Subtlety is required, but the business of meeting clients, launching products and promoting brands becomes more necessary and competitive when economies are suffering.

It is worth remembering that companies require aggressive marketing of their products and services, especially in times of hardship when competition stiffens. And, their staff need motivation during difficult times also. Sales conferences, product roadshows, product launches, album releases, fashion shows, concerts ... they all still happen when times are tough.

It may be that events are flashier and have larger attendances during good times, but less-good times do not equate to events not occurring.

There are downsides to choosing event management as a career. The job requires long days, long nights and unsociable hours. Often, an event organiser is working when other people are having fun. Most often, it is the event organiser who has organised that fun.

Event management is not a job with regular hours. Overtime payments are rarely made and there are no days off in lieu.

When an event enquiry comes in, the date of that event determines when the event organiser will be working. A client will not change the date of their event because the event organiser has a family engagement to attend.

Where there is diversity at one end of the event industry – being the sheer range of events, their creativity, and unlimited earning potential – it filters across to the other end, which means there are all sorts of opportunities to get into events. Events are everywhere where there is a live happening. And, you do not even need a qualification to get close to them. What better start could there be?

Chapter

The author's career path

Introduced by Olaf Olenski.

Philip Berners is an unusual event manager. By that I mean he has experience of most, if not all, sides of event management. This, in itself, is unusual.

I suspect it happened by accident, but Philip chose not to settle in one venue for the bulk of his career. Neither did he settle in one genre, such as producing events for the music industry or specialising in sports events.

Instead, Philip rose through the ranks at a time when nobody knew what events were or how to get into the business.

He diversified and has amassed a portfolio that includes venue management at Camden Palace, Thorpe Park and the famous London Hippodrome. He has acted as director of two event management companies, for which he won an industry award for Best Production Company. He also has experience of working as the head of events for large corporations where events were not the core business.

Crucially, Philip has been associated with and managed events that were large, small, high budget and low budget, charity and corporate, and of every known genre, including sports, fashion, music, conferences, launches, parties and awards.

It is this diversity and Philip's wealth of experience and knowledge in the field of event management that made me urge him to write this book, in the hope that it will provide Philip with a voice to be heard by those wishing to know something honest and informative about the management of events.

This is Philip's story . . .

•   •   •

'My pathway to event management was haphazard, but not untypical. It occurred in the days before managing events was considered a career. At that time there were no universities offering courses in event management.

At eighteen, I was already running six bars in a busy nightclub. I quickly moved to a job as the assistant manager at a member's-only leisure club in a magnificent country house, where I learnt the art of meeting customer expectations and maintaining exceptional standards of quality.

I completed a City & Guilds qualification in hotel and catering operations, only because my parents owned pubs and a small hotel. Thereafter, I achieved a degree in hospitality management at the University of West London.

My university work placement was at Thorpe Park where I conducted induction courses for summer seasonal staff. When my placement concluded, I received the award for student with the best work-related performance and was offered a chance to return to Thorpe Park once I had graduated. I did so and was offered the previous role, or the job of managing the cleaning department. I knew the cleaning department was poorly organised and inefficient. So, I took that challenge.

Running the cleaning in a 33-acre theme park with 1 million visitors a year presented daily difficulties that required swift management solutions. I was successful in raising the profile of the department and improving the cleaning standards to a level where it was minuted in the executive management meeting that standards were the highest since the park had first opened.

Presently, Thorpe Park asked me to run the events department, which was considered to be more in line with my university degree. Events were not the core business of the theme park and were considered an "add on". Even the staff were resistant to events happening because it interrupted their routine and often meant they needed to stay late. I remember feeling that I had been sidelined, if not demoted.

However, I applied high standards towards corporate clients, which included blue-chip organisations. Very quickly, the event business grew and was significantly contributing to the park's core revenue stream. Events became a stand-alone department with its own budget and target, so I began organising events during the closed season, such as Christmas parties. Mine was the only operational department over the winter months, which generated the only source of income to the business through the closed period.

By introducing the effective interdepartmental communication procedures that are now described in this book – primarily the event schedule and the pre-event briefing meetings – all other departments became engaged with the events at Thorpe Park. This allowed them to understand the challenges of meeting the needs and expectations of corporate clients who were paying for their event experience. This alone changed the organisational culture of the theme park, and the management and staff grew excited with new events. It reached a point where I was harangued to bring in more events to break the monotony of their everyday routine and provide staff with overtime.

I moved to the position of head of events at the London Hippodrome, which was a tired and dirty nightclub in Leicester Square. The venue had begun its life as a circus venue and the high corridors where the elephants were led in beneath the arena are still there today. Then, it became a music-hall theatre where Charlie Chaplin made his stage debut. The 1980s were the London Hippodrome's nightclub heyday under the stewardship of the legendary "King of Clubs", Peter Stringfellow. It became the hottest nightspot in London, frequented by Princess Diana and every pop star of the era.

By the time I reached it, the club's reputation was as smeared as its mirrors and chrome cladding. I recall that one of my corporate clients from the theme park said she was horrified that I was moving to such a dreadful venue and she would never use it. Perhaps, my decision was borne of my mother's philosophy that she would never take a good pub, because it can only go down. I was interested in venues where events were rock bottom and could only go upwards.

The scope of the Hippodrome and its West End location made it an exciting prospect for me. I relaunched the venue onto the corporate marketplace and highlighted its on-site facilities, capacity and flexibility for hosting large-scale events. I conducted an aggressive marketing campaign to change the perception of the venue being a dated nightclub. I then began to host corporate nights once a month for clients and event management agencies to get inside the place and witness its potential to host events. It was a thrill to surprise people at these intimate networking events where I could demonstrate the amazing sound, lighting, staging and special effects inherited from Mr Stringfellow.

Steadily, event business at the London Hippodrome grew from just four a year to over 100 and the profile of events increased too, with everything from a party for the Bee Gees to London Fashion Week. And, my once-horrified client from Thorpe Park placed two events with me at the Hippodrome.

A spell as the director of an event management company in Soho provided me with two high-profile restaurants in which to place events. This role also brought me into managing the artist facilities for three consecutive years at the massive BRIT Awards. During this spectacular event, I was responsible for the construction of the restaurant, bar and entertainment facilities for VIP guests and artists, and providing their hospitality needs. This provided a fascinating insight into the workings of an extremely high-profile event and took me into the company of Cher, Whitney Houston, David Bowie, Annie Lennox, Boy George, Robbie Williams, Eminem, Sting, U2 and Macy Gray.

Networking brought me a music label client who contracted me for the worldwide album launch of a Bon Jovi album, the post-Wembley party for Shania Twain and a private dinner for Reba McEntire.

About this time, I also produced a garden party in Windsor Great Park for Queen Elizabeth II, and film premiere parties and concert hospitality for the Prince's Trust.

I took the position as head of events for a company that published business magazines. My remit was to expand ten existing events that included industry awards, a trade conference, a high-level international golf tournament and an exhibitor party. Unfortunately, the culture was driven by cost, not creativity, so I left the company after delivering the largest awards ceremony in their history and increasing the revenue significantly by attracting a sponsor for the post-awards party.

I repeated the mistake by joining another publishing company: a newspaper publisher. They enticed me with an impressive list of advertisers as potential sponsors of events. I designed a remarkable event concept and achieved the impossible by receiving permission to close Leicester Square Gardens, which had never been done due to its status as a Royal Park. However, the newspaper's clients were space-bookers who were interested only in the position and size of page-spreads. So the potential for event sponsorship did not materialise and the inaugural event was cancelled.

In 2004, I relocated to Poland where I spent ten years as an event consultant, lecturer and director of the first event management school in Poland.

I returned to the UK and achieved Fellowship of the Higher Education Academy whilst lecturing in events management at the University of West London, from where I had graduated 22 years previously.

I intend to embark on a PhD to research the evolution of the events industry in a post-communist society: a case study of Poland. Currently, I teach hospitality and events management, and am the course co-ordinator for events management at the Edge Hotel School, University of Essex. Here, we blend theory with practical experience in our on-campus commercial hotel, Wivenhoe House. Finally, I am able to provide students with the learning and training they require to do the job of organising events.

My second book, *The Practical Guide to Managing Venues*, is in the process of being written.'

13.1 Author's eventography

(This list is not exhaustive.)

Table 3 Author's eventography

Queen Elizabeth II	Windsor	Garden party for members of the Royal Family and 500 guests. The Queen was host.
Prince Charles	London, Hyde Park	Artist and VIP hospitality at The Prince's Trust concert, including Blondie, Elvis Costello, Eurythmics
Prince Charles	London, Sugar Reef	Royal film premiere party for 'Notting Hill'
Princess Diana	London, Thorpe Park	Royal visit of Princess Diana with Princes William and Harry
The BRIT Awards	London	Artist and VIP hospitality for Cher, Whitney Houston, Sting, U2, Macy Gray, Boyzone, David Bowie, Westlife, Tom Jones, Steps, The Corrs, Annie Lennox, Robbie Williams, Eminem
The MOBO Awards	London, Royal Albert Hall	Artist hospitality for Tina Turner and Lionel Richie
Bon Jovi	Rome	Worldwide album launch, with VIP guests including Donatella Versace
William Hunt	London, Savile Row	Launch event of the fashion emporium
Jennifer Lopez	London, Leicester Square	Pan-European press launch
Reba McEntire	London, St James's Square	Private dinner and screening
Shania Twain	London, Home House	Post-Wembley party

The Bee Gees	London, The Hippodrome	Post-theatre premiere party
Xerox	London, Thorpe Park	Annual sales conferences
Mars Confectionery	London, Thorpe Park	Private hire nights
Philip Treacy	London, The Hippodrome	London Fashion Week
Home Entertainment	London, The Hippodrome	Magazine awards event
Max Power	London, The Hippodrome	Magazine awards event
PC Zone	London, Camden Palace	Magazine awards event
Licensed Trade Charity	London, The Hippodrome	Charity merger luncheon
Alternative Hair Show	London, Camden Palace	Hair fashion show
Kent Institute Art & Design	London, The Hippodrome	Graduate fashion show
Guildford College	London, The Hippodrome	Graduate fashion show
The British Red Cross	London, The Hippodrome	Opera speech, pre-show
The Publican Awards	London, Grosvenor House Hotel	Awards event for 2,000
Schweppes	London, Grosvenor House Hotel	Post-awards party
The Publican Newspaper	London, QEII Conference Centre	Business conference
The Publican Newspaper	Portugal	Golf tournament in the Algarve for top businessmen
Travelodge	London, Heathrow Airport	Hotel launch event
Diageo	London, Leicester Square	Christmas party

Appendix

Event enquiry form

See next page.

File Code:

Client Details: Name:

Address: Company Name: Position:

Email: Desk Phone: Mobile Phone:

Event Details:

Day & Date of Event: Number of Guests:

Location: Budget: £

Type of Event:
Conference / Meeting / Party / Banquet / Presentation / Wedding / Fashion / Other

Timings: Arrival / Departure

Catering Style: Lunch / Dinner / Banquet / Buffet / Canapés

Drinks: Reception / Bar (cash / credit) / Wines

Areas or Rooms Required:

Room Layouts:

Accommodation:

Other Requirements:

Action to take, and dates:

Date of Enquiry: Source of Enquiry: Taken by:

Appendix 11

Example sponsor packages

For the Happy Event Annual Awards

Title/Headline Sponsor (one available)

Value: 25,000

- Event title will incorporate the title sponsor's name
- Sponsor of the last category of award: the Lifetime Achievement Award
- Company representative to present award
- Photograph with caption for post-event press release
- Company logo on screen during presentation of award and during interval
- Company logo in prominent position on all printed material, including promotional posters, invitations, tickets, menus
- Company logo on venue branding, including on-stage, media photo wall, exterior branding
- Company portfolio inserted into guest gift bags
- Company portfolio available in press room
- Two tables, each of x10 guests.

Award Category Sponsors (nine available)

Value: 10,000

- Sponsor of award category
- Company representative to present award
- Company logo on screen during presentation of award and during interval
- Company logo on menus
- Company portfolio inserted into guest gift bags
- Company portfolio available in press room
- One table of x10 guests.

Satellite sponsors (five available)

Value: 5,000

- Company logo on screen during interval
- Company portfolio inserted into guest gift bags
- Company portfolio available in press room
- Company logo on menus
- One table of x10 guests.

Appendix

Event checklist

ITEM	WHO IS RESPONSIBLE	TICK WHEN DONE
SOUND		
Sound engineer		
DJ		
Band / Entertainment		
Sound equipment		
Microphones		
Public announcement system		
LIGHT		
Light engineer		
Lights for stage		
Lights for venue		
Lights for dance-floor		
Lights for exterior		
Gobos		
Follow spots		
Sky trackers		
Emergency lighting		

ITEM	WHO IS RESPONSIBLE	TICK WHEN DONE

POWER
Site electrician
Electricity
Water
Heating
Air conditioning
Waste

HEALTH & SAFETY
Medical box
Site nurse
Lifeboat and crew
Hazard analysis
Evacuation plan
Exit signage

TECHNICAL
Production manager
Pyrotechnics
Confetti cannons
Handheld radios
Talk-back

BARS
Bar manager
Bar service staff
Clearing staff
Stocking staff
Refrigeration
Beers
Wines
Spirits
Soft drinks
Juices
Ice
Towels
Oranges / Lemons / Limes /
    Pineapples
Straws
Corkscrews
Bottle openers

ITEM	WHO IS RESPONSIBLE	TICK WHEN DONE
Bins		
Glasses		
Knives		
Glass wash		
Ash trays		
Service trays		
Alcohol store		
Equipment store		

CATERING

ITEM	WHO IS RESPONSIBLE	TICK WHEN DONE
Catering manager		
Kitchen staff		
Service staff		
Clearing staff		
Dish wash		
Kitchens		
Refrigeration store		
Equipment store		
Food store		
Tables		
Chairs		
Cutlery & crockery		
Tablecloths		
Napkins		

SECURITY

ITEM	WHO IS RESPONSIBLE	TICK WHEN DONE
Security staff		
Car park staff		
Passes / Bracelets / Lanyards		
Guest list		
VIP list		
Press list		
Press barriers		
Perimeter fencing		
Metal screening		
X-ray screening		
Event photographer		
Courtesy umbrellas		
Taxi companies		
Velvet ropes		
Signage		

ITEM	WHO IS RESPONSIBLE	TICK WHEN DONE

CLOAKROOM
Cloakroom attendants
Coat racks
Bag racks
Umbrella stands
Numbered tickets
Full-length mirrors
Toilets
Toilet attendants
Fragrances
Hand towels

HOUSEKEEPING
Cleaners
Mops
Buckets
Dustpans
Brooms
Bins
Cloths

MARQUEE
Marquee structure
Marquee lining
Flooring
Carpeting

ON-SITE PRODUCTION OFFICE
Paper
Pens
Calculator
Stapler
Printer
Handheld radio chargers
Mobile phone chargers
First-aid box

ADDITIONAL ITEMS

Appendix

Administration checklist

ADMIN PROCECURE	DATE SENT OUT	DATE REC'D BACK	DONE
Enquiry form			
Proposal			
Confirmation			
Contact report			
Contract			
Signed contract			
Invoice			
Deposit			
Menu choice			
Final invoice			
Supplier 1			
Quote			
Order			
Deposit			
Balance			
Additional items			

Example function sheet (running order)

Event:	The Happy Event End of Year Conference
Date:	29 November
Brief:	The annual conference for Happy Event suppliers and contractors, to say thank you for their help and support during the year, and in preparation for the forthcoming busy Christmas season.

Guests will receive welcome drinks and canapés upon arrival, followed by a one-hour stage presentation. After the presentation, more drinks and canapés, and an informal networking party until the end.

DAY / TIME	ACTIVITY	WHO	CHECKED
Friday			
20:00	Deliver stage set to venue	Production	
Saturday			
06:00	Get-in.		
	Build stage	Production	
06:30	Sound installation	Production	
07:00	Light installation	Production	
08:00	Event Organiser on-site	Event Organiser	
08:00	Catering on-site	Catering	
08:15	Commence table set-up	Catering	
09:00	Theme and decoration	Decoration	
12:00	Lunch	All	
12:45	Standby for rehearsal	All	
13:00–14:00	Rehearsal		
16:30	Casual staff arrive	Catering	
17:00	All areas ready	All	
17:15	Staff briefing	Event Organiser	
17:30	Final venue walk-round	Event Organiser	
17:45	Security standby	Security	
17:45	Background lighting	Production	
17:45	Background music	Production	
18:00	Doors open	All	
18:00	Reception drinks service	Catering	
18:30	Reception canapé service	Catering	
18:55	Five-minute call	Production	
18:58	Two-minute call	Production	
19:00	Show start	Production	
19:45	Standby	Catering	
19:45	Standby	DJ	
20:00	Show end	Production	
20:00	Drinks service	Catering	
20:15	Canapé service	Catering	
22:00	End	All	
22:30	Commence de-rig	Production	
24:00	Venue clear	All	

Appendix  **VI**

Final report

See next page

EVENT DETAILS

Name of Event / Code No.:

Date of Event:

Venue:

Event Organiser:

List of Suppliers and Contractors:

POSITIVE ASPECTS TO REMEMBER

(Venue / Suppliers / Timings / Pre-event management / Operational event management /
Post-event management / Catering / Bars / Staffing / Access / Get-in / De-rig / Payments)

NEGATIVE ASPECTS TO REMEMBER

Glossary of technical terms

AAA (Access All Areas) A security pass or bracelet that allows someone access to all areas of the venue, including technical areas, front of house, backstage, kitchens and production rooms.

Backstage All areas of the venue behind the stage which are not visible or accessible to guests.

Band truck The moveable platform on a stage that houses the electronic elements of a band, most usually the drum kit.

Banqueting rounds / rounds Round tables with folding legs for easy storage. Used for banquets. 4 ft rounds will seat 6–8 diners, 5 ft rounds will seat 8–10 diners, 6 ft rounds will seat 10–12 diners and 6 ft trestles will seat 6 diners.

BOH (Back of House) All areas of the venue which are out of sight and inaccessible to guests.

Break-down The clearing-up period after the event.

Breakout room Meeting rooms used during conferences for splinter meetings or workshops. Separate from the main conference hall, but can be adjoining.

Cans The colloquial name given to headphones used for backstage and production crew.

Casual staff Temporary staff hired on an hourly basis, such as waiters and bar staff.

Catwalk The long section of stage for models to walk along at fashion shows.

Chafing dish A covered service dish used for keeping food warm on a buffet. A bath of water is heated by electricity or paraffin heaters underneath so as to keep the food hot.

Comfort break   The traditional period of relaxation towards the end of a formal meal (usually after coffee is served), when guests can visit the restroom, exit the venue to smoke, and gentlemen may remove their jackets.

COSHH   Care of Substances [that are] Hazardous to Health

Delegate rate   The all-inclusive charge per person (per delegate) charged for conferences. Typically, the delegate rate may include arrival coffee, mid-morning tea, lunch, afternoon tea and room hire fee.

De-rig   (see Break-down)

Dry ice   The fog effect used on stages.

Entertainment rider   The contractual requirements of an artist, presenter or performer.

Facility fee   The charge for hiring a venue.

F&B   Food & Beverage.

FH&S   Fire, Health & Safety.

Flats/silver flats   Trays from which to serve food. Used by waiters to serve canapés, or to display dishes on buffets.

Fog   The fog effect used from above the stage or auditorium, mainly to enhance laser and lighting effects.

FOH (Front of House)   All areas of a venue which are visible and accessible to guests.

Follow-spots   Lights that follow a person around the stage, or onto the stage. Operated by crew known as follow-spot operators.

Foreign consultant   A consultant with knowledge of the locality, particularly where events are held in foreign locations.

Genie   The machine that creates fog effects.

Gobo   A glass or metal disc which is inscribed with a logo or pattern and gets inserted into a light to project the effect.

Green room   A holding area backstage (and close to the stage) where guests are held before they appear on-stage. The green room is usually a hospitality area, but is also required to gather stage guests from other areas, such as dressing rooms.

Ground agent   (see Foreign consultant)

HACCP   Hazard Analysis and Critical Control Points

Hire fee   (see Facility fee)

Lanyard   A neck strap that holds a pass or identity card.

Lead-in The time leading up to the date of an event from confirmation to execution.

Load-in/Load-out (see Break-down)

MC (Master of Ceremonies) The person who presides over the formalities of an event and announces the speakers. The MC, or Toastmaster, should be a member of the Toastmasters International (TI) group and be liveried in a red-jacketed uniform.

Microphones

Desk mic	A microphone standing on a desk or table.
Handheld	A radio microphone held in the hand.
Head mic	A microphone worn on the head.
Lapel mic	A microphone worn on the lapel of a jacket.
Lead mic	A microphone with a cable.
Lectern mic	A microphone affixed to a lectern.
Radio mic	A microphone without a cable but with a short antenna.

Monitors

Comfort monitor	A television monitor that allows a speaker to see the screen presentation behind him (also known as a 'Stage vision monitor').
Ear monitors	Speakers worn inside the ear for a vocalist or musician to hear their performance.
Floor speaker monitor	Speakers on the floor of a stage for a vocalist or musician to hear their performance. Floor speaker monitors are referred to as 'wedges' because of their triangular shape.
Vision monitor	A closed-circuit television screen, usually used backstage to see what is happening on-stage.

Pitch / Pitching Open competition for winning an event job. The proposal will be *pitched* to the client.

Plate service The style of food service whereby waiters serve diners with the meal ready-plated.

Playback The backing music for a vocalist. Sometimes includes the voice in which case the vocalist will be miming their performance.

POS (Point of Sale) The place where a sale occurs. POS materials or POS merchandising are branded items placed where people make a purchase, such as on the bar top.

Production box The area where the production manager, sound engineer and light engineer are positioned. It is always positioned in front of the stage, so that these key members of production crew can view the stage.

Production manager The person in charge of the technical and stage elements.

Recce Reconnaissance.

Rental fee (see Facility fee)

RFI (Request For Information)   A speculative request from a client to receive information from prospective event organisers.

RFP (Request For Proposal)   A targeted request from a client for a proposal to be submitted by an event organiser.

Rider   (see Entertainment rider)

RSVP   *Répondez s'il vous plaît*, or *reply if you please* in relation to requesting a reply to an invitation.

Runway   (see Catwalk)

Show-caller   The person (usually the production manager) who 'calls' instructions to the technical crew during a show.

Silver flats   (see Flats)

Silver service   The style of food service whereby waiters serve with a serving spoon and fork.

Sky tracker   A skyward searchlight placed outside a venue to attract attention from afar.

Smoke   (see Dry ice)

Sprigs   Offshoot tables from a top table

Stage director   (see Production manager)

Stage wedge   (see Monitors; Floor speaker monitor)

Strike, or Striking   (see Break-down)

Talk-back   The communication system used by production and backstage crew, consisting of headphones and headset microphone.

Tech spec (Technical specification)   The list of technical requirements.

Toastmaster   (see MC)

Tray service   The style of food service whereby trays are placed onto the table for guests to help themselves.

Treads   Steps that lead up to a stage.

Trestles   Long tables with folding legs for easy storage.

'Triple A' Pass   (see AAA)

VIP   Very Important Person.

Voice of God   The public announcements made through a microphone or Tannoy system.

VVIP   Very, Very Important Person.

Wedges   (see Monitors; Floor speaker monitor)

Index

Taylor & Francis eBooks

Helping you to choose the right eBooks for your Library

Add Routledge titles to your library's digital collection today. Taylor and Francis ebooks contains over 50,000 titles in the Humanities, Social Sciences, Behavioural Sciences, Built Environment and Law.

Choose from a range of subject packages or create your own!

Benefits for you

» Free MARC records
» COUNTER-compliant usage statistics
» Flexible purchase and pricing options
» All titles DRM-free.

Benefits for your user

» Off-site, anytime access via Athens or referring URL
» Print or copy pages or chapters
» Full content search
» Bookmark, highlight and annotate text
» Access to thousands of pages of quality research at the click of a button.

REQUEST YOUR **FREE** INSTITUTIONAL TRIAL TODAY

Free Trials Available
We offer free trials to qualifying academic, corporate and government customers.

eCollections – Choose from over 30 subject eCollections, including:

Archaeology	Language Learning
Architecture	Law
Asian Studies	Literature
Business & Management	Media & Communication
Classical Studies	Middle East Studies
Construction	Music
Creative & Media Arts	Philosophy
Criminology & Criminal Justice	Planning
Economics	Politics
Education	Psychology & Mental Health
Energy	Religion
Engineering	Security
English Language & Linguistics	Social Work
Environment & Sustainability	Sociology
Geography	Sport
Health Studies	Theatre & Performance
History	Tourism, Hospitality & Events

For more information, pricing enquiries or to order a free trial, please contact your local sales team: www.tandfebooks.com/page/sales